THE OCCASIONAL COOK

Happy cooking, Janet!

♡ *Cyndy*

Sa

Eph 5:8

The Occasional Cook

Culinary Strategies for
Over-Committed Families

Cyndy Salzmann

HORIZON BOOKS

A DIVISION OF CHRISTIAN PUBLICATIONS, INC.
CAMP HILL, PENNSYLVANIA

HORIZON BOOKS

A DIVISION OF CHRISTIAN PUBLICATIONS, INC.
3825 Hartzdale Drive, Camp Hill, PA 17011
www.christianpublications.com

The Occasional Cook
ISBN: 0-88965-210-4
LOC Control Number: 2001-135746
© 2002 by Cyndy Salzmann
All rights reserved
Printed in the United States of America

02 03 04 05 06   5 4 3 2 1

To my children,
Freddy, Liz and Anna
for their love, encouragement
and willingness to try each one
of my dinnertime "experiments."

To my heavenly Father
for teaching me that even meat loaf
can be a powerful ministry.

Contents

Introduction

*"Say to wisdom, 'You are my sister,'
and call understanding your kins-
man." (Proverbs 7:4)*

Introduction

" They return at evening,
  snarling like dogs,
  and prowl about. . . .

They wander about for food
  and howl if not satisfied." (Psalm 59:14-15)

Does this sound like your home about 6 p.m.? Reading this verse still makes me shiver as I remember that "special" time each evening when the kids begin to whine, "What's for dinner, Mom? I'm hungrrrrryyyyy." Their persistent wail just exacerbated the guilt that (once again) I didn't have any specific plans. Unfortunately, my suggestion of "a nice bowl of Rice Krispies" generally didn't go over very well. Just as my pack of children would begin to circle for the kill, I'd grab the phone, call my husband and ask if he would mind picking up something for dinner on his way home from work.

I have to admit that my husband, John, appeared to be very understanding as I ticked off the many things that kept me from preparing dinner that day. However, I can still hear the edge of frustration in his voice as he said, "Don't worry about it, we can just order another pizza. Oh, Cyndy, I'm sorry. I didn't mean to say *another*." Talk about guilt! This was much worse than the howling of my children in the kitchen. And I don't even want to think about what all those pizzas and trips through drive-thru windows did to our budget—and to our waistlines.

Today, those times when I used to hover under that dark cloud of guilt because I couldn't get around to dinner have been virtually eliminated. Instead, when I have a busy day (and even when I don't), dinner is one thing I can quickly cross from my "to-do" list. Each morning, I take a meal from the many choices I have ready in the freezer. I might also toss some ingredients in the bread maker and set the timer so that the homey fragrance of a fresh loaf of bread is emerging from the oven at that "special" time of evening when the snarling and prowling is ready to begin. I've learned that a hot slice of home-baked bread will calm even the most savage beast.

I must confess, I don't expend the effort required by "occasional cooking" exclusively for the enjoyment of my husband and children. Frankly, I love to walk through the door after a long day knowing that dinner is ready to pop in the oven or toss on the grill. It's even nicer when the house smells like freshly baked bread. I can put my feet up and enjoy a cool drink or hot cup of tea before dinner instead of making a mad scramble to put something on the table. This is a much better start to the evening than passing around burgers and fries in the car or digging into rubbery pizza.

As my children get older, I've also begun to realize how quickly the years pass and the importance of taking advantage of every opportunity to spend time together. Even if we only have twenty minutes to sit down at the table before going our separate ways, dinner gives us a chance to reconnect. My husband and I often linger over a cup of coffee while the kids load the dishwasher. These days, they don't complain too loudly because there are few, if any, pots and pans to clean up. (Watch out, June Cleaver!)

A Reluctant Ant

"Go to the ant, you sluggard;
consider its ways and be wise! . . .
It stores its provisions in summer
and gathers its food at harvest."

(Proverbs 6:6, 8)

Just about now you might be saying, "Sounds good, but what's the catch?" Unfortunately, there *is* a catch. The bad news is that meals will not miraculously appear in your freezer—unless you can convince someone else to make them. The good news is that the process gets much easier each time you do it. You may not believe this after your first cooking day, but trust me, it's true.

I call my system for preparing meals in advance "The Occasional Cook." It follows the premise of the industrious ant who works hard to store food for the winter while the grasshopper plays in the sun. You can easily guess who will end up enjoying evenings by the fire while the other is knocking at the door of the anthill. I used to be the unhappy grasshopper (without even knowing it), but

for the last several years, I have found myself in the role of industrious ant.

Enough talk about insects. What am I really talking about? Basically, *The Occasional Cook* is a system where you spend about a day and a half every six weeks planning, shopping and preparing meals for the freezer. This allows you pretty much to cross "cook dinner" from your daily to-do list. Although I was a bit skeptical in the beginning, I have been cooking this way for several years and have become a true believer in its effectiveness.

Allow me to digress a moment to share a story that illustrates this point. Recently, I depleted my supply of meals, leaving only a lonely frozen turkey in the freezer. Since I had a full schedule for the next couple of weeks, I wasn't able to carve out a cooking day. We immediately found ourselves back in dinnertime crisis mode. It was miserable! We became so desperate that, one long weekend while I was home with the flu, my husband and children offered to provide the labor for cooking day while I supervised from the sofa. I must admit that this wasn't the most "bonding" family event, but we were all relieved when the freezer was full again.

A True Love-Hate Relationship

"He is wooing you from the jaws of distress
to a spacious place free from restriction,
to the comfort of your table laden
with choice food." (Job 36:16)

The Occasional Cook system works well for people who absolutely love to cook and those who absolutely hate to cook. How can this be? Let me explain.

There are times in my life when I love to cook. That's probably why I was initially attracted to the idea of preparing and freezing meals in advance. A full day in the kitchen didn't intimidate me . . . too much.

There are also times in my life when I absolutely hate to cook. Between volunteer activities, running my home business and shuttling children all over town, I am often too busy to shop, cook and (heaven forbid!) clean up the kitchen.

This love-hate relationship with cooking was the original impetus for my new vocation as an occasional cook. My family thought I was a bit crazy when I shared these plans with them. In fact, after cooking all day for the first time, I was so exhausted that I thought I might have bitten off more than I could chew (pardon the pun). I never again wanted to see another onion—much less sauté one. Nevertheless, after a good night's sleep, I began to feel a true sense of peace and accomplishment. I found myself staring in the freezer and marveling that I had thirty-six meals ready to go! I even called my husband and children to the garage to marvel with me. This didn't go over as well as I hoped. They were quite complimentary, but couldn't grasp the inexpressible joy I was experiencing with the realization that dinner was ready for at least six weeks!

As time went on, I found ways to streamline my cooking days using favorite family recipes. I began to include dinners for celebrations (birthdays, holidays, etc.) as well as extras like side dishes, desserts, cookies or muffins. It all depended on my mood and energy level.

Through the years, I have fine-tuned my method to meet the changing needs of our family. For example, we now follow a fairly low-fat diet, so many of the recipes I use reflect this change in lifestyle. Those of you with children know that as they grow, needs and schedules are constantly changing. I now incorporate simple meals (soup, sandwiches, etc.) or individual portions into my meal plan for particularly busy evenings. I also know the time will be soon upon us when I will be cooking for just myself and John. I know from experience (and the experience of other empty nesters) that I can easily adapt the system to this change. So, whether you are single or have a house full of little ones—I am confident you will be able to use *The Occasional Cook* to meet your needs.

Calm in the Midst of the Storm

"He has given food and provision to those who reverently and worshipfully fear Him."

(Psalm 111:5, AMP)

When we are obedient to God's prompting in our lives, He blesses us in so many ways. When it came to getting dinner on the table each evening, I literally felt the heavy hand of God weighing on my heart as I struggled to bring calm to this area of our lives. I give all praise and glory to Him for answering my cry for help. He has led me to wise people and helpful resources—as well as providing strength and encouragement to persevere. If you also struggle in this area, ask Him to do the same for you. You can trust Him to answer your prayer.

It's hard to believe all the blessings that have resulted from my occasional cooking. It has given me the freedom and time to do many things I truly enjoy, like spending the afternoon over tea with a friend or reading a good book, or going out to dinner with my husband while the kids eat a special "kids meal" I've tucked away in the freezer for them.

Even more importantly, being an "occasional cook" has given me the assurance that I am making good use of my time and resources. Just knowing that being a good steward in this area honors God and brings a deep sense of peace and joy!

> "And the Lord said, 'Who then is the faithful steward, the wise man whom his master will set over those in his household service, to supply them their allowance of food at the appointed time? Blessed—happy, and to be envied—is that servant whom his master finds doing so when he arrives.' "
>
> (Luke 12:42-43, AMP)

Basic Training

Much
More
Than
Food

"They broke bread in their homes and ate together with glad and sincere hearts." (Acts 2:46)

Much More Than Food

Why are *you* interested in learning *The Occasional Cook* system? I've asked this same question to the hundreds of people—single, married, parents, empty nesters or widowed—who have taken my occasional cooking workshop. Here's what they've told me:

- "Our family is always going in different directions. We have very little time to eat together—much less cook a meal."

- "I'm too tired when I get home from work to even think about cooking dinner."

- "I feel guilty when my husband gets home from work and I've been home with the kids all day and haven't gotten around to dinner."

- "We spend too much time and money in restaurants."

- "I am sick of fast food and pizza!"

- "We need to find a way to save money on groceries."

- "I can't remember the last time we sat down for a meal together. . . . I think it was Thanksgiving."

- "I am sick of cooking the same thing all the time. I need some new ideas!"

- "I don't feel like cooking for just myself."

- "I want to have tea at 4 o'clock like you do, Cyndy, instead of worrying about dinner!"

I must confess, several of these responses strike an uncomfortably familiar note with me. Many are the same reasons that attracted me to the idea of preparing and freezing meals in advance. These were the reasons I started using this system; but what has kept me cooking this way is much different—and is much more than food.

Building a Strong Family

"Unless the LORD builds the house,
  its builders labor in vain." (Psalm 127:1)

Recently, my son's school principal shared some pretty scary results from a survey that was conducted at his high school and at schools across the state in which we live. Of the 2,098 Nebraska young people surveyed in grades nine through twelve:

- 82% had drunk alcohol and 56% had done so in the last 30 days

- 46% had ridden in a car with a driver who had been drinking

- 26% had driven a motor vehicle after drinking alcohol in the last 12 months

- 65% had smoked a cigarette

- 31% had used marijuana

- 30% had been in a physical fight during the last 12 months
- 15% had carried a weapon in the past 30 days
- 17% had seriously considered committing suicide during the past 12 months

If these were national statistics, I probably would have just shaken my head and once again thanked God that we lived in Nebraska where I was certain very few teens would even think about participating in such risky behavior. As a mom, I had found it quite comfortable to keep my head in the sand. This time, however, I couldn't ignore the alarming results of this study that was conducted in my state and at my son's high school. To make things worse, I read in the January 29, 2001 issue of *Newsweek* magazine that there's been a steady increase in eating disorders, alcohol abuse and stress-related problems among teenagers.

About now, you may be thinking, "What does all this have to do with cooking?" The answer is "a lot." Research is demonstrating that sitting down to dinner together as a family on a regular basis has a profound impact on our children. And, no, it's not just because your children may be eating healthier foods or getting all their vitamins. The impact is much deeper. It goes to the heart of what we hope and pray for our children.

Dr. Blake Bowden of Cincinnati Children's Hospital Center conducted a study of 527 teenagers to determine what lifestyle characteristics were related to good mental health and adjustment. His research revealed that in families who eat dinner together at least five times a week, teens were least likely to become involved with drugs, feel depressed or get in trouble with police. They also were more likely to have better grades and a supportive circle of friends. These results contrast with the finding that the more poorly adjusted teens ate dinner with their parents three or fewer times a week. Dr. Bowden and his research team also found that having dinner together on a regular basis made more difference than age, gender or family type when predicting a teen's behavior. Wow!

> Having dinner together is of more value to a child's development than playtime, school and story time.

In 1996, Harvard professor Dr. Catherine Snow released the results of her study of sixty-five families over eight years. Her research revealed that having dinner together was of more value to a child's development than playtime, school and story time.

A 1993 *USA Today* poll found that one factor common to high achieving, well-adjusted adolescents was eating dinner with their families on a regular basis—even if the time at the table was as short as twenty minutes. Yet, less than one-third of families in the United States eat dinner together most nights.

Based on the results of these studies and others, the National Center on Addiction and Substance Abuse released in January 2001 a set of twelve parenting guidelines for raising drug-free kids. Among these guidelines to reduce the chance of teenagers smoking, drinking alcohol or using drugs is one which recommends that parents eat dinner with their children seven nights a week. Asked for a reaction to the guidelines, a teenager was quoted in our local newspaper as laughingly responding, "Yeah, right."

I must confess, if these guidelines were out a few years ago when I was miserably losing the daily battle to keep up with family demands, this news would have pushed me over the edge where I was already precariously perched. If you are also perched on that edge, I encourage you to first take a deep breath—then read on.

I am not sharing these statistics to heap on enough guilt to prod you into rushing to dust off your food processor and Crock-Pot. For the last several decades, society has diminished the role of work in the home. I think it is vitally important to understand the profound impact of what has been labeled "a mundane chore" on the lives of those closest to us. (And to think I was a woman who during high school wore a necklace with the word "Ms" and espoused an almost militant aversion to anything domestic.) The bottom line is that study after study has confirmed that the "old-fashioned" concept of the family dinner table needs to be reborn. Let it start in your home!

"She watches over the affairs of her household and does not eat the bread of idleness."

(Proverbs 31:27)

A Potful 'o Ministry Opportunities

"... their sorrow was turned into joy and their mourning into a day of celebration. He wrote them to observe the days as days of feasting and joy and giving presents of food to one another and gifts to the poor." (Esther 9:22)

It is easy to see how streamlining dinner preparation is a blessing to you and your family. I have also found, however, that my well-stocked freezer has been a powerful ministry to others. I always have a meal ready for a sick person or family in need, or I may use a meal to show appreciation to special teachers or a dear friend.

> God can use seemingly insignificant things to change lives, and it's important for us to be ready to act when He calls us.

Many of those who have attended my classes have been a wonderful encouragement by sharing examples of how they have used their occasional cooking to touch the lives of others. One woman told the story of how she sets aside a single portion of all the meals she prepares for her family to stock the freezer of a widow in her neighborhood. Another told how she made meals for a neighbor whose wife was undergoing cancer treatment and didn't have time to cook. I was also blessed to be part of a group of women in my church who came together to prepare meals for the families of our pastors as a way of showing our appreciation for their ministry.

Taking a meal to a family has also allowed me to unknowingly witness to strangers. The following story is a powerful example of how God can work if we are prepared and willing to take the opportunity He gives us. God can use seemingly insignificant things to change lives, and it's important for us to be ready to act when He calls us.

A few years ago, a woman from Florida visited a Bible study I was attending. She shared with our group that she had come to visit her parents. While here, her brother became suddenly and seriously ill. Sadly, he died the next day. When I found out, I offered to bring a meal to her family that evening. She said my offer would meet a great need since the family was still in a state of shock. I agreed to drop dinner by in a couple of hours and asked how many I should cook for. Her answer was, "about twenty-four people." I gulped and said I would see her soon.

Instead of going through my fried chicken coupons (a real temptation), I looked in the freezer. I spied three containers of home-made spaghetti sauce and began thawing them in the microwave. Next, I put some Italian bread in my bread-maker, threw together a salad (salad in a bag is such a blessing!) and began boiling pasta. While the bread baked, I had time to write a note of support and encouragement to the family. I delivered the food to a grieving group of peo-

ple that wondered what would motivate a stranger to prepare dinner for them.

About a month later, I received a beautiful note from the woman in Florida. She wanted me to know that my spaghetti dinner had been a powerful witness to her family. She said, "You can't know how your outpouring of love to complete strangers, with apparently nothing to gain, witnessed to my family, many of whom are unbelievers. They just couldn't understand why you would go to all that trouble for them. I had an opportunity to share Jesus with them when they saw how much He meant in your life. You brought much more than food to our family." And to think this resulted from less than an hour of my time that day! God truly works in wonderful ways!

Who in your circle of influence could benefit from your occasional cooking? Is it your husband, children, neighbor, pastor—or perhaps a single parent who could use some encouragement? Just remember, whether you are reaching in—or reaching out—your efforts for God's glory will make a positive difference in the lives of others.

"A generous man will himself be blessed. . . ."

(Proverbs 22:9)

The
Occasional
Cook
System

*"She sets about her work vigorously;
her arms are strong for her tasks."
(Proverbs 31:17)*

The Occasional Cook System

Are you ready? This chapter outlines the basic method for the system I call *The Occasional Cook*. It's important to remember, however, that the system is designed to fit the individual needs of the cook who is using it. As you work with it, you will find yourself adapting it in numerous ways. For example, you may follow the system as written and complete all of your meals in a day. Or you may spread the work out over two or three afternoons. I have even used the system to prepare Christmas cookies and breakfast entrees. Be creative!

Strong Arms

"Be strong and courageous." (Joshua 1:6)

The first time you cook may take a long time. Expect to get tired. The evening I finished cooking for the first time, I was certain nothing was worth the effort I had expended that day. I changed my mind after just a few evenings of reaping the rewards of my hard work (and sore back).

If you enjoy the system, you might want to add side dishes or breakfast dishes to your plan. I sometimes make cookie dough and freeze it in long rolls that are ready to slice and bake. (I really feel like June Cleaver when my kids can enjoy fresh-baked cookies after school. Maybe I should invest in some pearls!)

You may also choose to simplify the system with easy recipes and convenience foods which allow you to put together twenty to thirty meals in an afternoon. The key is to take the time at the start to learn the system and experiment until it works for you and your lifestyle.

Planning

"The fool folds his hands
   and ruins himself." (Ecclesiastes 4:5)

Planning is extremely important to the success of this system. Take it from a person who absolutely hates to plan. After many frustrating cooking days in the past, I now would much rather spend the time to plan than try to muddle through the mess a lack of planning makes in the kitchen.

Step 1: Choose the Basic Recipe

The first step is to gather several recipes for main entrees that you enjoy. As you will see from the recipes I have included in the following chapters, I like to use a basic recipe (stew, chili, etc.) and vary it with seasonings or use it several different ways. For example, I might triple my Basic Ground Meat Mixture (page 45) and use it to prepare Savory Meatloaf, Italian Meatball Grinders and Porcupine Stew. I also might decide to prepare a pot of Marinara Sauce (page 87) to use for

Lasagna, Linguine with Clams and Mexican Spaghetti. Get the idea?

I also often double or triple one of my family's favorite recipes. In fact, for the first few times you cook, I suggest sticking to family favorites. This helps to ensure that the response of your family is encouraging—not frustrating.

Try to select a mixture of dishes (chicken, beef, pork, fish, vegetarian, bean, cheese, egg). You will also want to vary the method of preparation somewhat. For example, you may want to include:

- meats that may be prepared on the grill or broiler (marinated chicken, shish kebabs)
- comfort foods (meatloaf, roast beef, chicken with gravy)
- stews or soups (beef bordeaux, chili, chicken soup, lentil or bean soup)
- casseroles or layered dishes (chicken divan, taco casserole, chicken enchiladas)
- sandwiches (sloppy joes, French dip, BBQ chicken sandwiches)
- pasta dishes (one or two sauces that can be used in a variety of ways)
- brunch-type dishes (quiche, egg casserole)
- kids' meals (make-your-own pizzas, macaroni and cheese casserole, chicken nuggets)

In my menu plan I almost always include a large pot of pasta sauce (usually marinara), soup (made from leftover vegetables and meat), a large beef roast (cooked in the Crock-Pot) and marinated chicken and/or fish. Be sure to select meals that fit into your lifestyle and dietary guidelines. If you follow a low-fat diet, select recipes that meet those requirements. Many favorite recipes can be modified with the variety of low-fat and fat-free products available today. For example, a quiche or egg casserole can be made using low-fat cheese and egg-product substitute in place of eggs. Many recipes that call for frying can be prepared with very little oil in a nonstick pan or cooked in the oven.

I almost always include one new recipe for my family to try each time I cook. When I serve it, the family is encouraged to make an honest assessment by voting thumbs-up, thumbs-down or so-so. This also helps me determine if the dish freezes well and what modifications need to be made to ensure quality. This process is very helpful when including meals in future menu plans.

A warning! Be careful about experimenting too much with new recipes or substitutions if you are doubling or tripling a recipe. You don't want to end up with three "disasters" in your freezer. If you are not sure about a recipe, my suggestion is to try one batch first. If it is a success, the next cooking day you may decide to double, triple or even quadruple it.

Step 2: Compile Ingredient Lists

After you have finalized your menu plan and determined how many of each recipe you will prepare, make a list of the ingredients. Remember to multiply each ingredient by the number of meals you plan to make with it. Next, combine common ingredients onto a master ingredient list. For example, I might have 10 cups of chopped onions on my master list.

I have found it easier to make a copy of each recipe, three-hole punch it and slip it into a binder. This is especially helpful when I plan to double or triple a recipe. I am able to calculate the ingredients for the number of meals and write the new proportions right on the copy in the binder. This system also frees me from having to flip through a cookbook or my recipe file on cooking day.

Step 3: Take an Ingredients Inventory

Check your pantry for the ingredients on your master list that you may already have on hand. Set them aside in a bag or on the counter. It is extremely important to actually check your pantry. On more than one occasion, I have been certain that I had an ingredient on hand but in the middle of cooking day could not locate it or found an empty box on the shelf. This has really thrown off the entire process—and aggravated my husband who is usually the one who runs to the store for me.

Step 4: Decide on Packaging

How do you plan to package and freeze each meal? List the packaging materials or containers in your notebook, pull them out and set them aside. Add anything you need to buy to your grocery list.

I use a lot of freezer bags (quart, gallon and 2-gallon sizes) because they take up less space. For example, I freeze meatloaf flat in 1-gallon freezer bag, put marinade in a bag and toss in frozen chicken breasts, and use bags for sliced meat and gravy, casseroles (not layered), hamburger patties, cheese or bread crumbs for toppings, etc. I use 2-gallon bags to group together several smaller bags for one meal. For example, you can put sloppy joes in one bag, buns in another and package both in one large 2-gallon bag. Bags also allow you to remove air and preserve the quality of the contents.

I freeze layered casseroles in baking dishes. It is a good idea to use dishes that can also be used in your microwave (glass, ceramic, etc.) in case you need to thaw or heat something quickly. I suggest putting pasta sauces and soups in plastic containers to prevent leakage. (You can also double bag to prevent this problem.) The key to preserving quality is to fit the container to the amount of food. Try to leave very little air space (1/4"-1/2"). Have a good permanent marking pen available to label and date all of your meals.

Step 5: Organize the Grocery List

The next step is to make a grocery list. Be sure to include all ingredients and packaging supplies. I organize the list by store (if I plan to use more than one) and department (meat, dairy, etc.). This cuts down on shopping time and leaves less possibility for forgetting a necessary ingredient. While you're at it, why not include something special to eat for lunch on your cooking day?

Step 6: Develop the Game Plan

Determine the best order to assemble and/or cook recipes and develop what I refer to as a "game plan" to guide you through your cooking day. The first tasks on my game plan include all prep work such as chopping, slicing, crushing, shredding and browning. Your plan should also include amounts to prepare such as "chop 10 cups of onions" or "shred 1 lb. of cheese."

At this point, you need to decide if you can include some convenience products to facilitate your cooking day. For example, my least favorite task is peeling and chopping onions. I especially hate the watery eyes that often go along with this chore. In fact, John once caught me wearing sunglasses in the kitchen while I chopped onions in an effort to keep my "weeping" to a minimum. One day, a friend introduced me to frozen, diced onions. Yippee! No more dicing onions for this cook! (By the way, I started comparing prices and found that cheese generally costs the same whether shredded or whole. I'm sure you can guess how I buy cheese now!)

Next, list on your game plan the assembly of slow-cooking items so they can simmer while you work on other meals. Then, list meals to assemble by categories (ground beef, marinated dishes, etc.). Finally, list the packaging of slow-simmering dishes that have cooled.

Putting together a detailed game plan is very important to the success of your cooking day. If it seems a bit daunting at first, be encouraged by the fact that the more you cook, the easier it will be to put together a plan. I have included sample menu plans, grocery lists and game plans in the Getting Started section (pp. 145-154) to help you get started. The plans are staggered from seven to twenty-one meals to "ease" you into the system.

The Day Before

"Much dreaming and many words are meaningless." (Ecclesiastes 5:7)

The work I plan for the day before my actual cooking day varies depending on my schedule. Since I rarely have a full day to cook anymore, I space the work over two or three afternoons. For example, I might do my shopping one day, do prep work and assemble slow-simmering dishes the next afternoon and finish assembling dishes the next day. Be flexible and it will be easier to work the system into your lifestyle. Remember, "occasional cooking" is designed to make your life easier—not make you a slave to the system. A note of caution: don't stretch out the process *too much* or you'll tire of all the tools and ingredients cluttering your kitchen.

Step 7: Go Shopping

After you have completed your meal list, game plan and grocery list, it's time to put your plan into action and hit the stores! I usually shop at three stores. First, I stop at a membership or warehouse store for bulk items such as frozen chicken breasts, large roasts, large cans of vegetables (tomatoes, etc.), dry beans, rice and some produce items (if quality looks good). I sometimes find good deals on freezer bags or plastic containers at a warehouse store too.

Next, I stop at a "no frills"-type store that offers discount prices in return for very little ambiance and service. This is where I purchase the remainder of the canned goods, frozen vegetables and dairy products as well as most of the meat and produce (depending on quality). There may be a few specialty items on my list that I will need to buy from a regular full-service grocery store. This is also a good place to pick up bakery and deli items you may need. And the butcher will be more willing to custom cut and slice your meat.

Shopping at more than one store is often the best way to save money, but sometimes there just isn't time to do it. I suggest doing what fits best with your time constraints and budget. Remember, this system is designed to save you time, not monopolize it.

Step 8: Unload and Assemble

As soon as you get home, unload the groceries. I unload directly onto the kitchen table so the ingredients are readily accessible. (All this food on the table also commits me to cooking!) Of course, I put away items that need to be refrigerated or frozen. Don't forget to defrost what you will need for your cooking day.

Next, set out all the packaging materials (ziplock bags, freezer containers, etc.) you will

need for the recipes you have selected. This is also a good time to pull out necessary pans, food processors, blenders, etc. The goal is to be ready to cook as soon as you reach the kitchen. I even get my morning coffee ready to brew!

Step 9: Pre-Cook What You Can

I usually do a little pre-cooking the afternoon or evening before cooking day. This helps me get started right away in the morning and makes the day run much more smoothly. For instance, I boil, skin and de-bone all the chickens so the meat is ready for recipes, and I put the broth in the refrigerator to chill. In the morning, I skim the fat from the top of the broth. With some leftover chicken and vegetables, this makes a great soup.

 Tip: If the fat from soup or broth is separated but not solid, remove fat by skimming the surface with a slice of bread.

I also sometimes put a roast in the Crock-Pot and turn it on low before I go to bed. In the morning, the meat is tender and juicy and ready to be packaged. This also frees the Crock-Pot for other uses during the day. (I picked up a second Crock-Pot at a garage sale. It is great for simmering spaghetti sauce, soup or stew without worrying about burning it.) And don't forget to soak dry beans overnight if you are using them.

Step 10: Get Set, Get Ready, Get Sleep!

With everything in place—ingredients, pots, pans, Crock-Pots and storage materials—you can go to bed and sleep in peace.

Cooking Day

"Worship the LORD your God, and his blessing will be on your food." (Exodus 23:25)

You've arrived! This is where the fun starts. You'll finally begin to see the fruit of your labor. To this day, I derive great satisfaction from watching the meals stack up in my freezer. It must be that "oil of joy" referred to in Hebrews 1:9!

Step 11: Fill Up the Sink

Fill up one side of your sink with warm soapy water. You will need to wash dishes as you cook throughout the day. This will keep the kitchen in order, and there will be less chance of confusion and/or contamination. I like to use an antibacterial dishwashing liquid and hand soap. Put on an apron (trust me, you will get messy) and pull out your game plan.

Step 12: Chop, Shred and Dice

The first list of tasks on your game plan should include chopping, shredding, dicing, crushing, etc. I have found that my food processor works very well for this. If you are using fresh chopped onions, keep them in a covered container in water to cut down on tears. Or you can avoid this problem completely by using frozen, diced onions.

As I peel and clean vegetables, I put all scraps (even the trimmings and skin and bones from meat) in a Crock-Pot turned on low. Add a little water and you will have a wonderful stock for soup or sauces at the end of the day. Just strain off the liquid, chill it and skim the fat. You can add leftover meat and/or vegetables to the stock for a tasty soup or use it in other recipes.

Tip: Rub your hands with salt to remove the smell of onions and garlic. Running them under cold water and rubbing a stainless steel spoon as you would a bar of soap will work too.

Tip: You can make fresh homemade bread crumbs from leftover bread using the meat blade of your food processor. Just put torn pieces of bread in the bowl, and let it whirl!

Step 13: Start the Simmering

Next, I start a large pot of spaghetti sauce and/or soup or stew simmering. Start these slow-cooking dishes or sauces early so they will be cool enough to package later. (Sometimes I prepare and cool them the day before to save time on my cooking day.)

Step 14: Start the Assembly Line

By now, you should be at the point of assembling other recipes, some of which are cooked, partially cooked or just ready-to-cook. It is a good idea to assemble the cooked dishes first so they have time to cool before packaging. Later, I assemble marinated dishes and casseroles that won't be cooked until the day they will be served.

 Tip: Using a tray, collect the ingredients you need before assembling a dish. When you are finished, put the ingredients aside. Repeat for the next dish on your game plan.

Step 15: Packaging

Package each meal after it has cooled. Be sure to label all packages with the name of the dish and the date. (It is amazing how different food looks after it has been frozen. I once made an accidental batch of Egg Drop Soup by pouring egg white [I had mistaken it for broth] into a simmering pot of chicken soup.) You may also want to write baking or cooking instructions for meals directly on the package. For example, "Bake 350° for one hour," or "Thicken simmering sauce with 2 T. of flour, pour over cooked noodles."

Step 16: Meal Inventory

Now to my favorite task on cooking day! Make an inventory list of the meals you have prepared. Isn't it fun to see what you have accomplished? Revel in the feeling for a bit, and then post the list in a convenient place. I put mine on the inside of a kitchen cupboard and cross off meals as I use them. Some cooks like to keep the list on the outside of their freezers. Just don't forget to revel!

Step 17: The Fun

Go out to dinner! You definitely deserve a break.

"Give her the reward she has earned,
    and let her works bring her praise."

(Proverbs 31:31)

Freezer
Facts

"This food should be held in reserve . . . to be used during the seven years of famine." (Genesis 41:36)

Freezer Facts

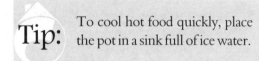

You're at the starting line, hunched down on your mark and ready to burst into the kitchen! Ready! Set! WAIT! Yes, WAIT! Before you take off on your occasional cooking adventure, spend a few minutes to review some basic rules on freezing food. After all, you'd hate to go through all the work and expense of preparing weeks worth of meals and have them emerge from the freezer as an unrecognizable mess that even the dog refuses to eat. But don't panic! I've found that freezing is probably the best way to preserve the natural flavor and texture of foods—if you know the tricks of the trade!

Be Quick!

"Everyone should be quick to listen."

(James 1:19)

Like any method of food preservation, freezing produces changes in food. When frozen, the water found in all foods forms ice crystals which can puncture cell walls. The faster you freeze a food, the smaller the ice crystals and, consequently, the less damage. Foods also release natural juices as they are thawed. This is why it's important to avoid partial thawing and refreezing. No one likes mushy food!

For the best quality, keep your freezer at 0°F. Although food may appear to be solidly frozen at 15° to 20°F, it will be of poorer quality when it is thawed. This is a good reason to consider investing in a separate freezer rather than using the freezer compartment of your refrigerator. It is difficult to maintain a constant temperature when the door is frequently opened. You can check the temperature of your freezer with a mercury-type freezer thermometer.

Do not place warm foods in the freezer. This will increase the temperature and affect the quality of food already frozen. Placing your meals directly next to the freezing plates or coils in the coldest part of the freezer will decrease freezing time. Also, try to leave enough space between packages for air to circulate. Once the packages are frozen, you can stack them closer together.

Tip: To cool hot food quickly, place the pot in a sink full of ice water.

I make it a habit to use all of the meals in my freezer before planning another cooking day. This way, I have an opportunity to defrost the freezer when it is least full. Built-up frost reduces storage space and raises the temperature of a freezer. You'll know it's time to defrost the freezer if frost is 1/4-inch thick.

To defrost your freezer quickly, first turn it off and prop the door open. Remove any food to another freezer or an insulated cooler. Place a large pot of boiling water in the freezer. While the steam begins to melt the ice, put another pot on the stove to boil. Keep switching the pots until all the ice has melted. Place a thick towel in the bottom of the freezer to soak up the water. Resist the temptation to chip away at built up frost with a sharp object (or any object, for that matter). This could damage the freezer coils.

After the ice has melted, clean your freezer with a solution of baking soda and warm water. Be sure to dry it thoroughly and wipe any moisture off packages before putting them back in the freezer. An opened box of baking soda in the back of the freezer will absorb odors.

Don't Get Burned

"Neither do men pour new wine into old wineskins. If they do, the skins will burst, the wine will run out and the wineskins will be ruined. No, they pour new wine into new wineskins, and both are preserved." (Matthew 9:17)

I can't say it more simply. Don't skimp on packaging. Your goal is to keep as much air as possible from food. Air changes the color, texture and flavor of food—commonly known as freezer burn. The way you package your meals and the quality of the material serves as protection from the damaging ef-

fects of air—and has a direct impact on the finished product.

You should use good quality packaging that is:

- vapor resistant
- water resistant
- durable
- pliable at low temperatures
- easy to seal
- appropriately sized

As I mentioned in the previous chapter, my top choice for packaging is a good quality freezer bag. I have tried to save money by purchasing store-brand or generic freezer bags and have been burned (freezer burned, that is) almost every time. The generic bags are almost always made of a thinner material and often seal poorly. Do not reuse freezer bags. Used bags invariably get tiny holes which let air into the package or allow liquid to leak out slowly, usually all over the freezer. Clip coupons if you like, but buy freezer bags of good quality.

A freezer bag will be of little use protecting your food if you don't remove as much air as possible. A neat trick is to seal the bag almost all the way, leaving an opening just large enough to slip in the tip of a straw. Use the straw to carefully suck out the air in the bag. Children *love* to do this!

Some dishes, such as layered casseroles, cannot be packaged in a freezer bag. Be sure to wrap these dishes tightly in heavy-duty aluminum foil. You can also use plastic containers, but be sure to fit the size to its contents. Leave 1/4 inch of head space for expansion during the freezing process.

Tip: Placing a sheet of plastic wrap directly on top of a dish before wrapping with foil or sealing with a lid will help to protect the food from freezer burn. Be sure to remove the plastic wrap before baking. (I'll never forget my "laminated" lasagna!)

Organize It!

"For God is not a God of disorder but of peace."

(1 Corinthians 14:33)

A freezer full of meals can quickly turn from a blessing to a burden if you can't find what you are looking for. After a few frigid experiences of digging through freezer bags to find an elusive package of meat loaf, I decided there had to be a better way. Now I organize my upright freezer by categories: comfort foods (meat loaf, soup, chicken and dumplings, roast, etc.) on the top shelf; ethnic dishes (chicken enchiladas, spaghetti and meatballs, etc.) on the second shelf; quick meals and single portions (sloppy joes, melts, hamburgers, etc.) on the third shelf; desserts and side dishes on the bottom shelf.

Some cooks color-code their meals with markers or labels. Just make sure you can see the label without pulling everything out. It's also a good idea to put new items in the back of the freezer and older ones in the front as a reminder to use them first. It's a bit more difficult to organize a chest-style freezer. One clever cook I know uses coated wire baskets. For example, one basket for meats, one for vegetables, etc. She can just pull out a basket to find what she is looking for instead of digging around inside. (By the way, she uses coated wire baskets because she found that plastic ones cracked in the freezer.)

The goal of developing a system to organize your freezer is to allow you to find what you need quickly. This will save time, help keep the freezer temperature constant—and, most importantly, prevent frostbitten fingers!

How Long Will It Keep?

"[H]e has given us . . . an inheritance that can never perish, spoil or fade."

(1 Peter 1:3-4)

Through the sacrifice of Jesus Christ, our inheritance as a child of God will never perish, spoil or fade. However, food will. Maintaining the proper temperature in the freezer and packaging meals appropriately is the best way to protect quality. How long they will maintain this quality depends on the type of food. My general rule is to make no more meals than can be used within two months. By following this guideline, I have had very few problems maintaining quality.

It is important to remember that you can thaw raw meat or poultry, cook it and then refreeze it. However, you cannot refreeze raw food without cooking it or refreeze cooked food that has been thawed. Does this make sense? If not, I suggest calling the experts with the U.S. Department of Agriculture Meat and Poultry Hotline at (800) 535-4555. Specialists are available Monday-Friday, 9 a.m.-3 p.m. CST, to answer your questions.

Quick
Tips

Quick Tips

Easy Lunch Ideas

- Spread cream cheese on tortillas. Layer on thin sliced deli meat such as ham, turkey or roast beef. Roll up tortillas, wrap individually in plastic and freeze together in a 1-gallon freezer bag. The roll-up will thaw in a couple of hours in a lunch box or a few seconds in the microwave. These make great after-school treats, too.
- Set aside individual portions from the meals you prepare on cooking day to use for a quick lunch or dinner.
- Set up an assembly line with family members in the kitchen to make sandwiches for the freezer. Use a variety of breads (bagels, rolls, etc.) and fillings.

Kitchen Safety

- Wash your hands thoroughly and frequently to prevent the spread of bacteria.
- Do not reuse dishes that held raw meat or poultry until they have been thoroughly washed with hot water and antibacterial soap.
- Cutting boards are notorious for cross-contamination. Disinfect a wooden cutting board (after using it

for raw meat or poultry) with hot water and a bleach solution. Allow the cutting board to air dry with the bleach solution. Then rinse with water.
- Keep the kitchen sponge from spreading germs by washing it in the dishwasher with the evening dishes.

Lean Cuisine

- Make recipes healthier by using no-fat or reduced-fat versions of ingredients such as sour cream, cheese, milk and ground meat.
- Using nonstick cookware allows you to cook with less fat.

Buddy System

- Cook with a friend.
- Split the cost, and split the meals.
- Time seems to fly with the buddy system—even God agrees!

"Two are better than one, because they have a good return for their work: If one falls down, his friend can help him up." (Ecclesiastes 4:9-10)

- Can't find a buddy who likes to cook? Turn on some upbeat praise music or check out a book on tape from your local library or Christian bookstore.

Spice It Up!

- Prepared sauces and spices easily change the flavor of a dish.
- Ginger and soy sauce add an oriental twist to meat and vegetables.
- Taco seasoning and salsa bring a bit of Mexico to your table.
- Spice blends like Cajun, Greek, Caribbean jerk and Mexican rubs can take your taste buds around the world.

New Life for Leftovers

- To get the most "bang for your buck," make every effort to tailor portions to fit your family size. If you end up with leftovers, give them new life with the following ideas:
  - chop up leftover meat loaf to use in spaghetti sauce (jar or home-made) or roll-up in a tortilla with lettuce, cheese and salsa for quick burritos.
  - cut leftover grilled chicken, beef or pork into strips. Add the meat to a bag of greens and some cheese to create a main dish salad.
  - make quick quesadillas by layering meat and cheese between two tortillas. Warm in a nonstick pan (or microwave) until cheese melts. Cut into wedges. Serve with sour cream and salsa.

- try adding leftover meat to stir-fry vegetables. Add a little teriyaki sauce. Serve with rice.

SECTION TWO

Recipes to Enjoy

Marinate It!

"Can something tasteless be eaten without salt?" (Job 6:6, NASB)

Marinate It!

Marinate It!

A marinade can add zest to an otherwise plain-Jane meal. Unfortunately, using a traditional marinade takes advance planning—anywhere from four to twenty-four hours to allow the flavor a chance to permeate the meat. Not anymore! By using the following method, your meat will marinate as it thaws—and be perfectly seasoned when you are ready to grill or broil it. You can also mix up a double or triple batch of marinade to use with different meats for a totally different taste—with a fraction of the effort! Each of the following recipes will yield enough marinade for one dish.

Savory Marinade
(chicken, pork, fish, beef, ground meat)

This is such a versatile marinade! It brings rave reviews when used with either chicken, fish, pork, beef or ground meat. You might even marinate cubed chicken, pork or beef for kebabs. To prepare kebabs for the grill or broiler after thawing, thread cubes on metal or wooden skewers with chunks of fresh vegetables such as mushrooms, zucchini, onions, peppers or cherry tomatoes. **Yield:** Approximately 1 cup.

Whisk together:
1 large clove garlic, crushed
1/2 cup oil
1/4 cup soy sauce
1 T. Worcestershire sauce
1/4 cup red wine vinegar
1/8 cup lemon juice
1 T. Dijon mustard
1/2 t. salt
1/2 t. pepper
1 T. parsley

Citrus Marinade
(fish, chicken)

This is a spunky marinade that's just right for a summer evening! Try it with fish or chicken and my favorite fruit salsa. (Combine a ripe, peeled, chopped mango with the juice of one lime and a tablespoon or so of fresh chopped cilantro. Olé!) **Yield:** 2/3 cup.

Whisk together:
1/4 cup lemon juice
1/8 cup lime juice
1/4 cup orange juice
2 T. oil
1 t. sugar
1/2 T. chopped cilantro

Honey Mustard Marinade
(chicken, pork)

This sweet and tangy marinade is sure to please your family!
Yield: 1 1/3 cups.

Mix together:
1/2 cup honey
1/4 cup Dijon mustard
1/4 cup lemon juice
1/4 cup soy sauce
2 cloves garlic, crushed

Teriyaki Marinade
(chicken, pork, fish, beef, ground meat)

A marinade with an Oriental twist. **Yield:** Approximately 1 cup.

Whisk together:
1/3 cup soy sauce
1/3 cup water
1/4 cup brown sugar
1 T. red wine vinegar
1 T. oil
1 clove garlic, minced
1 T. chopped chives or green onions

Using the Marinades:

For Chicken

Assembly: Place one recipe of marinade in 1-gallon freezer bag. Add 4-6 frozen chicken pieces. (Our favorite is boneless, skinless breasts.) Seal. Label. Place in freezer.
Preparation: Thaw chicken. Grill, brushing occasionally with marinade during first half of cooking.

For Pork

Assembly: Place one recipe of marinade in 1-gallon freezer bag. Add 4-6 pork chops or one boneless pork tenderloin. Seal. Label. Freeze.
Preparation: Thaw meat. Grill, brushing occasionally with marinade during first half of cooking.

For Fish

Assembly: Place one recipe of marinade in a small freezer bag. Place 4-6 fish filets in separate 1-gallon freezer bag. Place both bags into 2-gallon self-sealing bag. Seal. Label. Freeze.
Preparation: Thaw. Pour marinade over fish 10-30 minutes before grilling or broiling. Grill, brushing occasionally with marinade during first half of cooking. Cook fish just until it flakes.

For Beef

Assembly: Place one recipe of marinade in 1-gallon freezer bag. Add 1 to 1 1/2 lbs. sirloin steak, flank steak or London broil. Seal. Label. Freeze.

Preparation: Thaw. Grill to desired degree of doneness, brushing occasionally with marinade during first half of cooking. Slice thinly across the grain of the meat to serve.

For Ground Meat

Assembly: Mix 1/4 cup of marinade into up to 1 lb. of lean hamburger or other ground meat. Freeze flat in 1-gallon freezer bag. Place 4 hamburger buns in separate 1-gallon freezer bag. Place both bags in 2-gallon self-sealing bag. Label. Freeze.

Preparation: Thaw. Shape into patties. Grill until no longer pink in the center. Serve on buns.

Great
Ground
Meat

"The eyes of all look to you, and you give them their food at the proper time."

(Psalm 145:15)

Great Ground Meat

Great Ground Meat

Hamburger is about as American as apple pie, but unlike apple pie, there are countless variations on the theme. I have included two basic ground meat mixtures, one uncooked and the other fully cooked. My favorite recipes follow the instructions for each mixture. As always, however, I encourage you to experiment and adapt the mixes to your family favorites.

(NOTE: You may also substitute other ground meats, such as pork, turkey or chicken, for all or a portion of the beef; however, you will notice some variations in texture and flavor.)

• Basic Ground Meat Mixture (uncooked) •

1 1/2 lbs. lean ground beef
1 beaten egg or 1/4 cup egg substitute
3/4 cup soft bread crumbs
1/4 cup chopped onion
1/2 cup shredded carrots
1/2 t. salt
1/4 t. pepper

Gently mix all ingredients together. **Yield:** The above recipe provides the appropriate amount for one of the following recipes.

Tip: If you use chicken or turkey in your meat loaf, be sure to add some beef or pork. Using 100% poultry will result in a dry meat loaf.

Savory Meat Loaf

1 recipe Basic Ground Meat Mixture (uncooked)
1/4 cup milk
1 t. crushed (or 1 T. fresh) sage leaves
1/3 cup plus 2 T. catsup
3 T. brown sugar
1 T. prepared mustard

Assembly: Mix ground meat mixture, milk, sage leaves and 2 T. catsup together. Place in 1-gallon freezer bag and flatten. Mix remaining 1/3 cup catsup, mustard and brown sugar together. Place mixture in a small self-sealing bag. Seal both bags, removing as much air as possible. Place both bags in 2-gallon self-sealing bag. Label. Freeze.

Preparation: Thaw. Shape meat mixture into a 10 x 6-inch loaf and place on broiler pan. Bake at 350°F until no longer pink in the center, generally 45-60 minutes. During last 10 minutes, top with sauce.

Tip: Use your hands to mix meat loaf, but don't work the mixture too vigorously or your finished product will be tough.

Italian Meat Loaf

1 recipe Basic Ground Meat Mixture (uncooked)
1/4 cup milk
2 t. fennel seed
1 large clove garlic, crushed
1 cup marinara sauce (page 87) or your favorite
  meatless spaghetti sauce
1 cup shredded mozzarella cheese

Assembly: Mix ground meat mixture, milk, fennel seed and garlic. Place in 1-gallon freezer bag and flatten. Place shredded cheese and marinara sauce in separate 1-quart freezer bags. Seal all bags, removing as much air as possible. Place bags in 2-gallon self-sealing bag. Label. Freeze.

Preparation: Thaw. Shape meat mixture into a 10 x 6-inch loaf and place on broiler pan. Bake at 350°F until no longer pink in the center, generally 45-60 minutes. During the last 10-15 minutes, top meatloaf with marinara sauce and sprinkle with shredded mozzarella cheese.

Tip: Italian meat loaf is wonderful with Garlic Mashed Potatoes. Just spice up your regular mashed potato recipe by tossing a few peeled cloves of garlic into the water while you cook the potatoes. Mash the garlic right along with the potatoes.

Southwestern Meat Loaf

1 recipe Basic Ground Meat Mixture (uncooked)
1/4 cup milk
1 large clove garlic, crushed
1 cup salsa (hot, medium, mild, according to your taste)
1 cup shredded cheddar or jack cheese

Assembly: Mix ground meat mixture, milk, garlic and 1/2 cup salsa. Place in 1-gallon freezer bag and flatten. Place shredded cheese and remaining salsa in separate 1-quart freezer bags. Seal all bags, removing as much air as possible. Place bags in 2-gallon self-sealing bag. Label. Freeze.

Preparation: Thaw. Shape meat mixture into a 10 x 6-inch loaf and place on broiler pan. Bake at 350°F until no longer pink in the center, generally 45-60 minutes. During the last 5-10 minutes, top meat loaf with salsa and sprinkle with shredded cheese.

Tip: Leftovers are great wrapped in warm tortillas. Top with cheese, shredded lettuce, sour cream and chopped tomatoes.

Nebraska Shepherd's Pie

1 recipe Basic Ground Meat Mixture (uncooked)
1 t. crushed sage leaves
1/4 cup milk
2 T. catsup
3 cups mashed potatoes (see Tip)
2 cups frozen country vegetables (green beans, corn
   and carrots)
1 cup shredded cheddar cheese

Assembly: Mix ground meat mixture, milk, sage leaves and catsup. Place in 1-gallon freezer bag and flatten. Place cheese and frozen vegetables in separate 1-quart freezer bags. Seal all bags, removing as much air as possible. Place all bags in 2-gallon self-sealing bag. Label. Freeze.

Preparation: Thaw. Spray an 8 x 8-inch baking dish with cooking oil. Press meat mixture into the pan. Bake at 350°F until no longer pink in the center, generally 25 minutes. Pour off fat and drippings. While meat is cooking, cook and drain vegetables (generally 4-5 minutes in the microwave). Mix cooked vegetables, cheese and warm mashed potatoes. Spread mixture on top of meat and bake for 10 minutes until cheese melts.

 Tip: Freezing potatoes is always tricky business and mashed potatoes are no exception. The defrosted product may be somewhat runny. I've solved this problem by heating the thawed mashed potatoes in the microwave for 5-6 minutes, uncovered. This seems to bring back the original consistency. You can avoid this problem entirely by using either instant mashed potatoes or the frozen mashed potatoes available at your grocery store. In this case, just prepare the required amount when you plan to serve this dish. (Of course, you can also prepare homemade mashed potatoes on the day you plan to serve the meal!)

Caribbean Meat Loaf

1 recipe Basic Ground Meat Mixture (uncooked)
1/4 cup milk
2 t. jerk seasoning
1 large clove garlic, crushed
1 8-ounce can crushed pineapple (drained)
1 9-ounce jar mango chutney
1 T. chopped fresh mint (or 1 t. dried)
1 small jalapeño pepper, finely chopped (optional)

Assembly: Mix ground meat mixture, milk, jerk seasoning and garlic. Place in 1-gallon freezer bag and flatten. Mix pineapple, chutney, mint and jalapeño pepper (if desired). Place mixture in a 1-quart freezer bag. Seal both bags, removing as much air as possible. Place bags in 2-gallon self-sealing bag. Label. Freeze.

Preparation: Thaw. Shape meat mixture into a 10 x 6-inch loaf and place on broiler pan. Bake at 350°F until no longer pink in the center, generally 45-60 minutes. During last 15 minutes, top loaf with 1/2 cup of the pineapple mixture.

Italian Meatball Grinders

1 recipe Basic Ground Meat Mixture (uncooked)
1/4 cup milk
2 t. fennel seed
1 large clove garlic, crushed
2 cups marinara sauce (page 87) or your favorite
    meatless spaghetti sauce
1 cup shredded mozzarella cheese
4 large Italian hoagie rolls

Assembly: Mix ground meat mixture, milk, fennel seed and garlic. Shape into 2-inch meatballs. Bake meatballs at 400°F until no longer pink, generally 20 minutes. (Use a broiler pan to allow extra fat to drain away.) Cool meatballs and transfer to 1-gallon freezer bag. Pour marinara sauce over the meatballs. Place shredded cheese in separate 1-quart freezer bag and rolls in another 1-gallon freezer bag. Seal all bags, removing as much air as possible. Place all bags in one 2-gallon self-sealing bag. Label. Freeze.

Preparation: Thaw. Simmer meatballs and sauce until heated through. Heat rolls in 400°F oven for 5-7 minutes. Split rolls, top with hot meatballs and sauce. Sprinkle with mozzarella cheese.

Porcupines

1 recipe Basic Ground Meat Mixture (uncooked)
1/4 cup uncooked long-grain white rice
   (not Minute Rice™)
2 1/2 cups beef broth
1 6-ounce can tomato paste
1/4 cup brown sugar, firmly packed
1/4 cup red wine vinegar

Pantry:
3-4 cups shredded red cabbage (small head)

Assembly: Mix ground meat mixture and rice. Shape into 1-inch meatballs. Bake meatballs at 400°F about 10 minutes. (Use a broiler pan to allow extra fat to drain away.) Cool meatballs and transfer to 1-gallon freezer bag. Add remaining ingredients (except cabbage) to freezer bag. Seal bag, removing as much air as possible. Place all bags in a 2-gallon self-sealing bag. Label. Freeze.

Preparation: Thaw. Simmer meatballs and sauce, covered for 25 minutes. Add shredded cabbage and simmer for an additional 10 minutes.

Sweet and Sour Meatballs

1 recipe Basic Ground Meat Mixture (uncooked)
1 8-ounce can water chestnuts, drained and chopped
1/4 cup milk
1 T. Worcestershire sauce
1/2 cup lemon juice
1/4 cup catsup
1/2 cup brown sugar, firmly packed
1/4 t. salt
2 T. cornstarch
1 cup chopped red or green pepper

Assembly: Mix ground meat mixture, water chestnuts, milk and Worcestershire sauce. Shape into 1-inch meatballs. Bake meatballs at 400°F about 10 minutes. (Use a broiler pan to allow extra fat to drain away.) Cool meatballs and transfer to 1-gallon freezer bag. In a small pan, combine remaining ingredients (except pepper). Cook and stir over medium heat until sauce thickens. Add pepper and simmer 5 minutes. Cool sauce, then add to freezer bag with meatballs. Seal bag, removing as much air as possible. Label. Freeze.

Preparation: Thaw. Simmer meatballs and sauce, uncovered until heated through. This dish can be used as a main course, served with fried rice or as an appetizer.

Swedish Meatballs

1 recipe Basic Ground Meat Mixture (uncooked)
1/2 cup chopped dill pickle
3/4 cup milk
1/4 t. ground nutmeg
1 10 1/2-ounce can cream of mushroom soup

Assembly: Mix ground meat mixture, dill pickle, 1/4 cup milk and nutmeg. Shape into 1-inch meatballs. Bake meatballs at 400°F about 10 minutes. (Use a broiler pan to allow extra fat to drain away.) Cool meatballs and transfer to 1-gallon freezer bag. Mix soup and remaining 1/2 cup milk and add to freezer bag Seal bag, removing as much air as possible. Label. Freeze.

Preparation: Thaw. Simmer meatballs and sauce uncovered until heated through. This dish can be used as a main course or as an appetizer. If served as a main course, it is wonderful served over egg noodles. (Our favorite noodles are the frozen variety.)

BBQ Meatballs

1 recipe Basic Ground Meat Mixture (uncooked)
1/4 cup milk
1 t. minced garlic
1 cup barbeque sauce

Assembly: Mix ground meat mixture, milk and garlic. Shape into 1-inch meatballs. Bake meatballs at 400°F about 10 minutes. (Use a broiler pan to allow extra fat to drain away.) Cool meatballs and transfer to 1-gallon freezer bag. Add barbeque sauce to freezer bag. Seal bag, removing as much air as possible. Label. Freeze.

Preparation: Thaw. Simmer meatballs and sauce uncovered until heated through. This dish can be used as a main course or as an appetizer for a party. If used as main dish, my family likes to pair the meatballs with macaroni and cheese.

Pizza Burgers

1 recipe Basic Ground Meat Mixture (uncooked)
2 t. fennel seed
1 large clove garlic, crushed
1 cup marinara sauce (page 87) or your favorite
   meatless spaghetti sauce
1 cup shredded mozzarella cheese
4 hamburger buns or Italian rolls

Assembly: Mix ground meat mixture, milk, fennel seed and garlic. Place in 1-gallon freezer bag and flatten. Place shredded cheese and marinara sauce in separate 1-quart freezer bags. Place hamburger buns or rolls in another 1-gallon freezer bag. Seal all bags, removing as much air as possible. Place all bags in one 2-gallon self-sealing bag. Freeze.

Preparation: Thaw. Shape meat mixture into hamburger patties. Grill or broil until no longer pink in center. Heat rolls in 400°F oven for 5-7 minutes. Split rolls, top with burgers and 1/4 cup sauce. Sprinkle with mozzarella cheese.

Zesty Burgers

1 recipe Basic Ground Meat Mixture (uncooked)
1 T. prepared horseradish
2 t. Dijon mustard
1/2 t. paprika
4 hamburger buns

Assembly: Mix ground meat mixture, horseradish, mustard and paprika together. Place in 1-gallon freezer bag and flatten. Place hamburger buns or rolls in another 1-gallon freezer bag. Seal both bags, removing as much air as possible. Place bags in one 2-gallon self-sealing bag. Label. Freeze.

Preparation: Thaw. Shape meat mixture into hamburger patties. Grill or broil until no longer pink in center. Heat rolls in 400°F oven for 5-7 minutes. Split rolls and top with burgers.

55

• Basic Ground Meat Mixture (cooked) •

1 lb. lean hamburger
1/2 cup chopped onion (1 medium)
1 t. minced garlic
1/2 t. salt
1/2 t. pepper

Brown meat, onion and garlic until meat is no longer pink. Drain fat. **Yield:** Approximately 3 cups.

Cheeseburger Casserole

1 recipe Basic Ground Meat Mixture (cooked)
8 ounces processed cheese, cubed
1/3 cup catsup
8-ounce package of elbow macaroni, cooked *al dente*
1 cup chow mein noodles (or other topping)

Assembly: Mix ground meat mixture, cheese, catsup and macaroni. Place in 1-gallon freezer bag, gently flattening. Place chow mein noodles in a smaller freezer bag. Seal both bags, removing as much air as possible. Place bags in 2-gallon self-sealing bag. Label. Freeze.

Preparation: Thaw. Put mixture in baking dish. Heat in 350°F oven, uncovered until heated through. Top with chow mein noodles during last 5 minutes.

Tip: You'll know your casserole is heated through when it begins to bubble around the edges.

Popover Pizza

1 recipe Basic Ground Meat Mixture (cooked)
3 cups marinara sauce (recipe on page 87) or your
     favorite meatless spaghetti sauce
2 cups shredded mozzarella cheese

Pantry:
1 tube refrigerated crescent rolls
1/4 cup Parmesan cheese

Assembly: Place ground meat mixture and sauce in 1-gallon freezer bag, gently flattening. Place cheese in a smaller freezer bag. Seal both bags, removing as much air as possible. Place bags in 2-gallon self-sealing bag. Label. Freeze.

Preparation: Thaw. Put meat and sauce mixture in a 9 x 5-inch baking dish. Top with shredded mozzarella cheese. Unroll crescent roll dough and fit on top of casserole. Sprinkle with Parmesan cheese. Bake at 375°F for 30-35 minutes until crust is golden and filling is hot.

Tip: Food baked in a glass dish cooks more quickly than in a metal pan. Lower your baking temperature 25° or more when using a glass pan.

Mexi-Melt

1 recipe Basic Ground Meat Mixture (cooked)
1/2 cup salsa (mild-hot according to taste preference)
1 15-ounce can refried beans
1 cup shredded cheddar or jack cheese

Pantry:
tortillas or tortilla chips
salsa
sour cream

Assembly: Mix ground meat mixture and salsa. Spray an 8 x 8-inch baking pan with cooking oil. Layer meat mixture, beans and finish with cheese. Cover tightly. Label. Freeze.

Preparation: Thaw. Heat in 350°F oven, loosely covered until heated through. Serve with tortillas or chips, salsa and sour cream.

Chuck Wagon Quesadillas

1 recipe Basic Ground Meat Mixture (cooked)
1 t. chili powder
1 t. ground cumin
1 9-ounce can baked beans
1 8-ounce can diced tomatoes with green chilies
1 cup frozen corn
2 T. barbeque sauce
4 large flour tortillas
1 1/2 cups shredded cheddar or jack cheese

Assembly: Mix all ingredients except tortillas and cheese. Place in 1-gallon freezer bag, gently flattening. Place tortillas in separate 1-gallon freezer bag. Place cheese in a smaller self-sealing bag. Seal all bags, removing as much air as possible. Place bags in 2-gallon self-sealing bag. Label. Freeze.

Preparation: Thaw. Lightly coat nonstick skillet with cooking spray. Lay one tortilla in skillet. Top with warmed meat mixture, sprinkle with cheese. Repeat layers two more times, and end with tortilla to top stack. Cover and cook over low heat until cheese melts and stack is hot in center. (You may microwave this instead, but we enjoy the crispiness of the bottom tortilla when it is heated in the skillet.) Cut in wedges and serve with sour cream, shredded lettuce, salsa, etc.

Easy Enchiladas

1 recipe Basic Ground Meat Mixture (cooked)
1 31-ounce can refried beans
1 19-ounce can enchilada sauce
3 cups shredded cheddar or jack cheese
4 large flour tortillas cut or torn into strips

Assembly: Spray an 9 x 5-inch baking pan with cooking oil. Coat bottom of pan with thin layer of enchilada sauce. Layer half of the tortillas, meat, beans and 1/3 cheese. Cover with 1/2 remaining enchilada sauce. Repeat layers with remaining tortillas, meat, beans and sauce. Finish with remaining cheese. Cover tightly. Label. Freeze.

Preparation: Thaw. Bake at 350°F, loosely covered until heated through. Serve with sour cream, salsa, sliced olives, chopped tomatoes and shredded lettuce, if desired.

Zesty Beef and Noodles

1 recipe Basic Ground Meat Mixture (cooked)
1 cup salsa
1 8-ounce package of noodles, cooked *al dente*
1 t. chili powder
2 14-ounce cans cream-style corn
1 cup crushed cornflakes (or other topping)

Assembly: Mix ground meat mixture, salsa, noodles, chili powder and corn. Place in 1-gallon freezer bag, gently flattening. Place cornflakes in a smaller freezer bag. Seal both bags, removing as much air as possible. Place bags in 2-gallon self-sealing bag. Label. Freeze.

Preparation: Thaw. Put casserole in baking dish. Heat in 350°F oven, uncovered until heated through. Top with cornflakes during last 5 minutes.

Tip: Be careful not to overcook pasta. Start tasting after six minutes. Remove when the pasta is *al dente*—literally, "to the tooth" in Italian. It will be soft but firm at the center when you taste. Immediately stop the cooking process by draining the pasta and thoroughly rinsing with cold water.

Calico Beans

1 recipe Basic Ground Meat Mixture (cooked)
1/4 cup cooked, crumbled bacon
1/2 cup catsup
1 T. mustard
1 T. vinegar
3/4 cup brown sugar
1 16-ounce can kidney beans (drained)
1 16-ounce can pork and beans
1 16-ounce can lima beans

Assembly: Combine all ingredients. Place in 1-gallon freezer bag, gently flattening. Label. Freeze.

Preparation: Thaw. Put casserole in baking dish. Heat in 350°F oven, uncovered until heated through, about 45 minutes. This may be served as a main dish or a side dish at a barbeque or picnic.

Captain's Stew

1 recipe Basic Ground Meat Mixture (cooked)
4 cups beef broth
1 16-ounce package frozen country vegetables
    (green beans, carrots, corn)
1 16-ounce can diced tomatoes (undrained)
1 16-ounce can kidney beans (drained)
1 cup vegetable juice
1 t. marjoram
1 t. oregano
1 t. thyme
1 t. sugar

Assembly: Mix all ingredients. Place in 1-gallon freezer bag. Seal bag, removing as much air as possible. Place bag in another 1-gallon bag to prevent leakage. Label. Freeze.

Preparation: Thaw. Pour stew in pot and simmer 20-25 minutes. Season with salt and pepper to taste.

Taco Soup

1 recipe Basic Ground Meat Mixture (cooked)
1 package dry taco seasoning
2 cups beef broth
1 16-ounce can diced tomatoes
1 16-ounce can diced tomatoes with green chilies
2 16-ounce cans kidney beans, drained
2 cups frozen corn
1 T. sugar
1 cup shredded cheddar cheese
3-4 cups tortilla chips

Assembly: Mix all ingredients except cheese and tortilla chips. Place soup in 1-gallon freezer bag. Seal bag, removing as much air as possible. Place bag in another 1-gallon bag to prevent leakage. Place cheese in a smaller self-sealing bag. Place tortilla chips in 1-gallon freezer bag. Place all bags in 2-gallon self-sealing bag. Label. Freeze.

Preparation: Thaw. Pour soup in a large pot and simmer 20-25 minutes. To serve, place several slightly crushed tortilla chips in bottom of each bowl. Ladle soup over chips. Top with cheese. Serve with sour cream, salsa, and chopped green onions on the side, if desired.

Tastee Joes

1 recipe Basic Ground Meat Mixture (cooked)
1 T. vinegar
3/4 cup catsup
1 T. brown sugar
1 t. mustard
4-6 hamburger buns

Assembly: Mix all ingredients (except hamburger buns) together and place in 1-gallon freezer bag. Place hamburger buns or rolls in separate 1-gallon freezer bag. Seal both bags, removing as much air as possible. Place bags in 2-gallon self-sealing bag. Label. Freeze.

Preparation: Thaw. Simmer meat mixture on medium-low heat for 15-20 minutes, uncovered. Serve on warm hamburger buns.

BBQ Cups

1 recipe Basic Ground Meat Mixture (cooked)
1 cup barbeque sauce
1 cup shredded cheddar cheese

Pantry:
2 tubes large (or giant-sized) refrigerated biscuits

Assembly: Place meat mixture and barbeque sauce in 1-gallon freezer bag. Place cheese in a smaller self-sealing bag. Seal both bags, removing as much air as possible. Place bags in 2-gallon self-sealing bag. Label. Freeze.

Preparation: Thaw. Warm meat mixture until heated through. Press biscuits onto the bottom and up the sides of greased muffin cups. Spoon 2-3 T. of meat mixture into each muffin cup. Bake at 375°F 15 minutes or until golden brown. Top with cheese during last 5 minutes.

Italian Biscuit Cups

1 recipe Basic Ground Meat Mixture (cooked)
1 1/2 cups marinara sauce (recipe page 83) or your
    favorite meatless spaghetti sauce
1 cup shredded mozzarella cheese

Pantry:
2 tubes large (or giant-sized) refrigerated biscuits

Assembly: Place meat mixture and marinara sauce in 1-gallon freezer bag. Place cheese in a smaller self-sealing bag. Seal both bags, removing as much air as possible. Place bags in 2-gallon self-sealing bag. Label. Freeze.

Preparation: Thaw. Warm meat mixture until heated through. Press biscuits onto the bottom and up the sides of greased muffin cups. Spoon 2-3 tablespoons of meat mixture into each muffin cup. Bake at 375°F 15 minutes or until golden brown. Top with cheese during last 5 minutes.

International
Stew

*"She is like the merchant ships,
bringing her food from afar."
(Proverbs 31:14)*

International Stew

International Stew

These recipes were a lot of fun to develop and a big hit at my cooking workshops, never failing to bring a chorus of "ohhh's" and "ahhh's" from participants.

The basic mixture is a snap—one of those "dump-and-forget-it" recipes. The fun comes when you begin to assemble the dishes and find yourself caught up in a culinary world tour just by adding just a few ingredients to the basic recipe.

One note of caution: although these recipes are meant to be assembled directly into the freezer bag, they will need 20-30 minutes to simmer and meld flavors on the day you serve them. So be patient, and enjoy your trip around the world!

• Basic Braised Beef Mixture •

4-5 lbs. boneless stew meat (lean)
2 T. minced garlic
6 cups beef broth (or whatever fits in your Crock-Pot)
3 cups chopped onions

Put all ingredients in a Crock-Pot. Cook on low overnight (10-12 hours) or high (5-6 hours).
Yield: Enough beef and broth for four recipes.

Beef Bordeaux

3-4 cups Basic Braised Beef Mixture
1 package frozen baby carrots
1 cup sliced mushrooms
1/2 t. each: salt, pepper, thyme
1 cup beef broth
1 cup unsweetened red grape juice
1 package frozen egg noodles

Pantry:
2-3 T. flour

Assembly: Place all ingredients, except noodles, in 1-gallon freezer bag. Seal bag, removing as much air as possible. Place bag and noodles in 2-gallon self-sealing bag. Label. Freeze.

Preparation: Thaw. Simmer stew 20-25 minutes. Cook noodles. When stew is bubbling, thicken with 2-3 tablespoons of flour. Adjust seasonings. Serve over cooked noodles. Garnish with chopped parsley. Voilà!

Beef Stroganoff

3-4 cups Basic Braised Beef Mixture
2 cups sliced mushrooms
1/2 t. each: salt, pepper
1 1/2 cups beef broth
1 package frozen egg noodles

Pantry:
1 8-ounce sour cream
2 T. flour

Assembly: Place all ingredients, except noodles, sour cream and flour in 1-gallon freezer bag. Seal bag, removing as much air as possible. Place bag and noodles in 2-gallon self-sealing bag. Label. Freeze.

Preparation: Thaw. Simmer stew 20-25 minutes. Cook noodles. Thicken simmering stew with flour. Adjust seasonings. Stir in sour cream. Serve over cooked noodles. Garnish with chopped parsley, if desired.

Tip: Instant potato flakes can thicken sauces, soups and stews.

Osso Bucco

3-4 cups Basic Braised Beef Mixture
1 package frozen baby carrots
1 16-ounce can diced tomatoes
1/4 t. each: basil and thyme
1 cup unsweetened white grape juice
1 package risotto

Assembly: Place all ingredients except risotto in 1-gallon freezer bag. Seal bag, removing as much air as possible. Place bag and package of risotto in 2-gallon self-sealing bag. Label. Freeze.

Preparation: Thaw. Simmer stew 20-25 minutes. Adjust seasonings. Serve over risotto which has been prepared according to package directions. Garnish with chopped parsley, if desired.

Middle Eastern Stew

3-4 cups Basic Braised Beef Mixture
1 8-ounce can tomato sauce
1/2 cup water
1/4 t. each: ginger, cinnamon, nutmeg
2 t. each cumin, oregano
2 cups frozen carrots
1 bag frozen spinach
1 package couscous
1/2 cup raisins

Assembly: Place all ingredients except couscous and raisins in 1-gallon freezer bag. Place raisins in a small self-sealing bag. Seal bags, removing as much air as possible. Place both bags and package of couscous in 2-gallon self-sealing bag. Label. Freeze.

Preparation: Thaw. Simmer stew 20-25 minutes. Adjust seasonings. Prepare couscous according to package directions. Stir in raisins. Serve with stew.

Southwestern Stew

3-4 cups Basic Braised Beef Mixture
1 16-ounce package frozen corn
small bunch chopped cilantro
3 t. cumin
1/4 t. red pepper
2 t. sugar
2 cans Mexican-style tomatoes
1 16-ounce can red kidney beans
1 cup long-grain rice

Assembly: Place all ingredients except rice in 1-gallon freezer bag. Put rice in a small self-sealing bag. Seal both bags, removing as much air as possible. Place both bags in 2-gallon self-sealing bag. Label. Freeze.

Preparation: Thaw. Simmer stew 20-25 minutes. Adjust seasonings. Meanwhile, mix rice with 2 cups water, 1 t. butter or margarine and 1/2 t. salt. Simmer until water is absorbed and rice is fluffy. Serve stew over cooked rice. Garnish with chopped parsley, if desired.

Oriental Stew

3-4 cups Basic Braised Beef Mixture
1 16-ounce package frozen stir-fry vegetables
1 bunch green onions, sliced
1 t. each: grated orange peel, ginger
1/2 cup stir-fry sauce
1 cup long-grain rice

Assembly: Place all ingredients except rice in 1-gallon freezer bag. Put rice in a small self-sealing bag. Seal both bags, removing as much air as possible. Place bags in 2-gallon self-sealing bag. Label. Freeze.

Preparation: Thaw. Simmer stew 20-25 minutes. Adjust seasonings. Meanwhile, mix rice with 2 cups water, 1 t. butter or margarine and 1/2 t. salt. Simmer until water is absorbed and rice is fluffy. Serve stew over cooked rice. Garnish with additional sliced green onions, if desired.

Orange Beef and Rice

3-4 cups Basic Braised Beef Mixture
1 cup sliced mushrooms
1 cup shredded carrots
1/2 t. Italian seasoning
1 cup orange juice
1 t. grated orange rind
1/2 cup water
1 6-ounce package white and wild rice pilaf mix

Assembly: Place all ingredients except rice in 1-gallon freezer bag. Seal bag, removing as much air as possible. Place bag and package of rice mix in 2-gallon self-sealing bag. Label. Freeze.

Preparation: Thaw. Simmer stew until bubbling. Add rice pilaf mix and simmer until liquid is absorbed.

Swiss Steak

3-4 cups Basic Braised Beef Mixture
1 cup frozen sliced carrots
1/2 cup sliced celery
1 16-ounce can diced tomatoes
1/4 t. each: basil and thyme

Assembly: Place all ingredients in 1-gallon freezer bag. Seal bag, removing as much air as possible. Label. Freeze.

Preparation: Thaw. Simmer stew 20-25 minutes. Adjust seasonings. Serve with mashed potatoes.

Chill Out

"By the sweat of your brow you will eat your food." (Genesis 3:19)

Chill Out

Chill Out

OK, I admit it. I don't think a pot of chili is worth its beans if it doesn't make you sweat—at least a little. However, my recipe has much more than the sweat on my husband's brow to recommend it. This chili swept the awards at my daughter's youth group chili cook-off—garnering everything from "Best Recipe" to "True Blue Belly Bomber."

I also use this recipe for much more than just chili. It makes a great taco salad, Mexican casserole, huevos rancheros, chili pie, queso dip—the possibilities are endless. How many ways can you think of to use this "True Blue Belly Bomber"? (My address and e-mail are at the back of the book.)

• Basic Recipe: Cyndy's Chili •

1 recipe Basic Ground Meat Mixture
   (cooked—recipe on page 56)
1 package chili seasoning mix
1 green pepper, chopped
3 16-ounce cans chopped tomatoes
4 16-ounce cans dark red kidney beans
1 15-ounce can tomato sauce
1 cup of water
1 1/4 t. coarse black pepper
3/4 t. chili powder
1 1/2 t. ground cumin
1 t. salt
2 T. sugar
1/2 t. red pepper (depending on taste)

Combine seasonings and mix into meat mixture. Add remaining ingredients. Cook on stove at low heat for at least 60 minutes, stirring frequently. Chili is better if simmered 2-3 hours. (You can also simmer this in a Crock-Pot on low for 4-6 hours or longer.) Adjust seasonings. Cool. **Yield:** 12 cups.

Chili 'n Cheese

8 cups Cyndy's Chili
1 1/2 cups shredded cheddar cheese
6-8 flour tortillas

Assembly: Place chili and tortillas in separate 1-gallon freezer bags. Put cheese in a small self-sealing bag. Seal all bags, removing as much air as possible. Place bags in 2-gallon self-sealing bag. Label. Freeze.

Preparation: Thaw and heat chili over low heat. Garnish bowls with cheddar cheese. Serve with warm tortillas.

Southwestern Bakers

3 cups Cyndy's Chili
1 1/2 cups shredded cheddar cheese

Pantry:
4 large baking potatoes
salsa
sour cream

Assembly: Place chili and cheese in separate 1-quart freezer bags. Seal bags, removing as much air as possible. Place bags in 2-gallon self-sealing bag. Label. Freeze.

Preparation: Prick and bake potatoes at 350°F until soft (or cook in microwave). Thaw and heat chili. Top potatoes with warm chili and cheese. Garnish with salsa and sour cream.

Taco Salad

3 cups Cyndy's Chili
1 1/2 cups shredded cheddar cheese
3-4 cups tortilla chips

Pantry:
1 bag salad greens
salsa
ranch dressing

Assembly: Place chili, chips and cheese in separate 1-quart freezer bags. Seal bags, removing as much air as possible. Place bags in 2-gallon self-sealing bag. Label. Freeze.

Preparation: Thaw and warm chili. Mix ranch dressing with 2-3 tablespoons salsa and toss greens with this mixture. Place dressed greens in serving dish. Top with chips, warm chili and cheese. Garnish with salsa and sour cream.

Mexican Salad

3 cups Cyndy's Chili
1 1/2 cups shredded cheddar cheese
3-4 cups tortilla chips

Pantry:
1 bag salad greens
1/2 cup Catalina dressing

Assembly: Place chili, chips and cheese in separate 1-quart freezer bags. Seal bags, removing as much air as possible. Place bags in 2-gallon self-sealing bag. Label. Freeze.

Preparation: Thaw chili. Mix cool chili and the remaining ingredients with salad greens and Catalina dressing. Salad may be served slightly chilled or at room temperature.

Taco Casserole

3 cups Cyndy's Chili
1 1/2 cups shredded cheddar cheese
3-4 cups tortilla chips

Pantry:
lettuce
salsa
sour cream

Assembly: Place chili, chips and cheese in separate 1-quart freezer bags. Seal bags, removing as much air as possible. Place bags in 2-gallon self-sealing bag. Label. Freeze.

Preparation: Thaw chili. Place slightly crushed chips in 9 x 5-inch baking dish. Top with chili, then cheese. Bake at 350°F until heated through, 20-25 minutes. Top with lettuce. Garnish with salsa and sour cream.

Cheesy Chili Mac

3 cups Cyndy's Chili
1 package macaroni and cheese mix
1 cup shredded cheddar cheese

Pantry:
salsa
sour cream

Assembly: Place chili and cheese in separate 1-quart freezer bags. Seal bags, removing as much air as possible. Place bags and macaroni and cheese mix in 2-gallon self-sealing bag. Label. Freeze.

Preparation: Thaw chili. Prepare macaroni and cheese according to package directions, except cook the macaroni noodles *al dente.* Mix chili with prepared macaroni and cheese. Top with shredded cheese. Bake at 350°F until heated through, about 20 minutes. Garnish with salsa and sour cream.

Chili Dogs

3 cups Cyndy's Chili
1 cup shredded cheddar cheese
1 package 8-10 hot dogs
1 package 8-10 hot dog buns

Assembly: Place chili and cheese in separate 1-quart freezer bags. Place hot dog buns in 1-gallon freezer bag. Seal bags, removing as much air as possible. Place bags and package of hot dogs in 2-gallon self-sealing bag. Label. Freeze.

Preparation: Cook hot dogs according to package directions on grill or in microwave. Thaw and heat chili. Place hot dogs in buns and top with warm chili and cheese.

South-of-the-Border Pie

3 cups Cyndy's Chili
1 cup shredded cheddar cheese
1 8.5-ounce box cornbread mix

Pantry:
1 8-ounce can corn (drained)
1 8-ounce can cream-style corn

Assembly: Place chili and cheese in separate 1-quart freezer bag. Seal bags, removing as much air as possible. Place bags and cornbread mix in 2-gallon self-sealing bag. Label. Freeze.

Preparation: Thaw chili. Prepare cornbread mix according to package directions, except add corn and cream-style corn to mix. Spray 9-inch pie plate with cooking oil. Place half of the cornbread mixture in the prepared pan. Top with chili, then cheese. Finish with remaining cornbread mixture. Bake pie at 400°F for approximately 30-35 minutes or until cornbread is deep golden brown. Cut into wedges to serve.

Jorge's Favorite Queso Dip

2 cups Cyndy's Chili
1 8-ounce processed cheese, cubed

Pantry:
1 t. liquid smoke
1 bag tortilla chips

Assembly: Place chili and cheese in 1-gallon freezer bag. Seal bag, removing as much air as possible. Label. Freeze.

Preparation: Thaw. Heat chili and cheese mixture in the microwave, fondue pot or Crock-Pot until melted. Stir in liquid smoke. Serve dip with tortilla chips.

Huevos Rancheros

4 cups Cyndy's Chili
1 cup shredded cheddar cheese
6-8 flour tortillas

Pantry:
8-10 eggs (uncooked)

Assembly: Place chili and tortillas in separate 1-gallon freezer bags. Put cheese in a small self-sealing bag. Seal all bags, removing as much air as possible. Place bags in 2-gallon self-sealing bag. Label. Freeze.

Preparation: Thaw. Heat chili in a 12-inch nonstick frying pan until bubbling. Crack eggs into simmering chili without breaking yolks. Cover and cook until egg white is set and yolk is still soft (or to desired degree of doneness). Carefully remove egg and spoonful of chili from pan to warmed plate. Serve with tortillas and hot sauce, if desired.

Southwestern Spaghetti

3 cups Cyndy's Chili
3 cups marinara sauce (see recipe page 87 or use
    your favorite meatless spaghetti sauce)
1 cup shredded cheddar cheese
1 8-10 ounce package of spaghetti

Assembly: Place chili and marinara in 1-gallon freezer bag. Place cheese in a smaller self-sealing bag. Seal bags, removing as much air as possible. Place both bags and spaghetti in 2-gallon self-sealing bag. Label. Freeze.

Preparation: Thaw. Heat chili and marinara mix together until warmed through. Meanwhile, cook spaghetti according to package directions. Serve sauce over hot pasta. Top with shredded cheese.

Shortcut Tamales

3 cups Cyndy's Chili
1 1/2 cups shredded cheddar cheese
3-4 cups corn chips

Pantry:
salsa
sour cream

Assembly: Place chili, chips and cheese in separate 1-quart freezer bags. Seal bags, removing as much air as possible. Place bags in 2-gallon self-sealing bag. Label. Freeze.

Preparation: Thaw. Place slightly crushed chips in 8- or 9-inch pie plate. Top with chili, then cheese. Bake at 350°F until heated through, 20-25 minutes. Garnish with salsa and sour cream.

That's Italian!

"Two are better than one, because they have a good return for their work: If one falls down, his friend can help him up."

(Ecclesiastes 4:9-10)

That's Italian!

That's Italian!

I grew up in St. Louis surrounded by some great Italian cooks, so it's no surprise that one of the staples of my menu plan is a thick and flavorful marinara sauce. Some even call marinara sauce "Italian gravy"—and I can see why. It tastes great on just about anything! As an added bonus, unlike most gravies, my marinara is low in fat and calories and loaded with vitamins.

Every Italian cook has his or her version of a marinara—which is basically a tomato-based sauce without meat. It can be thick or thin, chunky or smooth. I prefer marinara as a basic sauce as opposed to a meaty "sugo" (which means "tomato sauce with meat") because it is more versatile. I can easily transform marinara into a meat sauce by adding hamburger, Italian sausage or any combination of ground meats. Marinara is also easily transformed into a red clam sauce with the addition of clams. I can add vegetables for a yummy primavera sauce, serve it over stuffed shells or manicotti, or whip up a layered baked pasta loaded with creamy cheese. As my favorite Italian cook, Clarenzo, says, *"Mangia!"* (Let's eat!)

• Basic Marinara Sauce •

6 large cloves garlic (minced)
1 1/2 cups diced onion
3 T. olive oil
1 large can crushed tomatoes (6 lbs., 4 oz.)
1 large can diced tomatoes (6 lbs., 4 oz.)
1 14-ounce can tomato paste
2 T. sugar
3 T. oregano leaves
3 T. basil leaves
1 t. pepper
1 t. salt (or to taste)

Sauté garlic and onion in olive oil until translucent. Add rest of ingredients. Simmer for as long as you want, at least 2 hours. Taste and adjust seasonings. **Yield:** 15 cups

Tip: To release flavor, rub dried herbs between your fingers before adding.

Spaghetti with Sugo Sauce

4-6 cups Basic Marinara Sauce
1 lb. Italian sausage, hamburger or other
 ground meat, cooked and drained
1 8-ounce package spaghetti (or your favorite pasta)

Assembly: Place marinara sauce and cooked ground meat in 1-gallon freezer bag. Seal bag, removing as much air as possible. Place bag and package of pasta in 2-gallon self-sealing bag. Label. Freeze.

Preparation: Thaw. Prepare pasta according to package directions. Meanwhile, simmer sauce until heated through. Serve pasta topped with sauce. Garnish with Parmesan cheese and chopped parsley, if desired.

Spaghetti with Meatballs

4-6 cups Basic Marinara Sauce
1 recipe Italian Meatball Grinders (meatballs only)
1 8-ounce package spaghetti (or your favorite pasta)

Assembly: Place marinara sauce and cooled meatballs in 1-gallon freezer bag. Seal bag, removing as much air as possible. Place bag and package of pasta in 2-gallon self-sealing bag. Label. Freeze.

Preparation: Thaw. Prepare pasta according to package directions. Meanwhile, simmer sauce until heated through. Serve pasta topped with sauce. Garnish with Parmesan cheese and chopped parsley, if desired.

Linguine with Red Clam Sauce

4 cups Basic Marinara Sauce
1 6-ounce can clams, drained
1 8-ounce package linguine (or your favorite pasta)

Assembly: Place marinara sauce and clams in 1-gallon freezer bag. Seal bag, removing as much air as possible. Place bag and package of pasta in 2-gallon self-sealing bag. Label. Freeze.

Preparation: Thaw. Prepare pasta according to package directions. Meanwhile, simmer sauce until heated through. Serve pasta topped with sauce. Garnish with Parmesan cheese and chopped parsley, if desired.

Penne with Parma-Rosa Sauce

3 cups Basic Marinara Sauce
1/4 cup grated Parmesan cheese
3/4 cup heavy cream
1 8-ounce package penne pasta (or your favorite pasta)

Assembly: Mix marinara sauce, cheese and cream. Place in 1-gallon freezer bag. Seal bag, removing as much air as possible. Place bag and package of pasta in 2-gallon self-sealing bag. Label. Freeze.

Preparation: Thaw. Prepare pasta according to package directions. Meanwhile, simmer sauce until heated through. Adjust seasonings. Serve pasta topped with sauce. Garnish with Parmesan cheese and chopped parsley, if desired.

Pasta Primavera

4 cups Basic Marinara Sauce
1-2 cups assorted sliced vegetables:
    mushrooms, green or yellow peppers, snow peas,
    broccoli, cauliflower
1-2 T. olive oil
1 8-ounce package rigatoni (or your favorite pasta)

Assembly: Sauté vegetables in olive oil for 2-3 minutes. Place marinara sauce and cooled sautéed vegetables in 1-gallon freezer bag. Seal bag, removing as much air as possible. Place bag and package of pasta in 2-gallon self-sealing bag. Label. Freeze.

Preparation: Thaw. Prepare pasta according to package directions. Meanwhile, simmer sauce until heated through. Serve pasta topped with sauce. Garnish with Parmesan cheese, if desired.

Family Pizza

1 pizza shell
1 1/2 cups Basic Marinara Sauce
1 cup mozzarella cheese
 3-4 ounces pepperoni or other cooked meat

Assembly: Package marinara sauce, cheese and meat in separate 1-quart freezer bags. Place all bags and wrapped pizza shell in 2-gallon self-sealing bag. Label. Freeze.

Preparation: Thaw. Spread sauce on pizza shell. Top with meat and cheese. (You may also choose to add some additional fresh vegetables at this time, such as sliced mushrooms, chopped green pepper, onion, etc.) Bake at 375°F for 10-15 minutes until cheese is melted and begins to bubble. Serve immediately.

Baked Pasta

8 ounces cooked penne pasta, cooked *al dente*
4-6 cups Basic Marinara Sauce
12 ounces ricotta cheese
1 egg or 1/4 cup egg substitute
1/2 cup Parmesan cheese
1 1/2 cups mozzarella cheese

Assembly: Mix together ricotta, egg and Parmesan cheese. Spread 1/3 of the marinara sauce in bottom of casserole dish that has been sprayed with cooking oil. Add 1/2 of cooked pasta. Spread cheese mixture over pasta. Cover with 1/3 of sauce. Add rest of pasta. Cover with remaining sauce. Cover tightly with foil. Put mozzarella cheese in 1-quart freezer bag. Attach to casserole with tape or rubber band. Label. Freeze.

Preparation: Thaw casserole. Bake covered at 350°F for 40-45 minutes until bubbly. Uncover. Top with cheese and bake for an additional 5 minutes.

Tip: No need to worry if your dish bubbles over in the oven. Just sprinkle salt on the spill and finish baking. When the dish is done, the salt will have turned to ash, and the spill will be a snap to clean up.

Old-Fashioned Lasagna

8 ounces lasagna noodles, cooked *al dente*
4-6 cups Basic Marinara Sauce
1 recipe Basic Ground Meat Mixture, cooked
    (see recipe on page 56)
12 ounces ricotta cheese
1 egg or 1/4 cup egg substitute
1/4 cup Parmesan cheese
2 t. dried parsley flakes
salt and pepper to taste
1 1/2 cups mozzarella cheese

Assembly: Mix together ricotta, 1 cup mozzarella cheese, Parmesan cheese, egg, parsley and seasonings. Mix cooked meat mixture and marinara sauce. Spray a 13 x 9 x 2-inch casserole dish with cooking spray. Spread 1 cup of the meat sauce. Place three strips of pasta lengthwise over the sauce. Spread 1/2 of the ricotta mixture over the pasta. Cover with 1 1/2 cups meat sauce. Repeat layers of pasta, ricotta mixture and meat sauce. Top with remaining pasta, meat sauce and mozzarella cheese. Cover tightly with foil. Label. Freeze.

Preparation: Thaw casserole. Bake covered at 350°F for 30 minutes. Remove foil and bake an additional 15 minutes until hot and bubbly. Let stand 10 minutes before serving.

 Tip: Lasagna can be baked from a frozen state. It will take from 45-60 minutes longer. However, I prefer it thawed, then baked.

Tallerina

1 recipe Basic Ground Meat Mixture, cooked
  (see recipe on page 56)
2 1/2 cups Basic Marinara Sauce
1 8-ounce package of wide noodles, cooked *al dente*
1 T. chili powder
1 14-ounce can cream-style corn
6 ounces processed cheese, cubed
1/4 cup French-fried onion rings

Assembly: Mix ground meat mixture, marinara sauce, noodles, chili powder, corn and cheese. Place in 1-gallon freezer bag, gently flattening. Place onion rings in a smaller freezer bag. Seal both bags, removing as much air as possible. Place bags in 2-gallon self-sealing bag. Label. Freeze.

Preparation: Thaw. Put casserole in baking dish. Heat in 350°F oven, uncovered until heated through. Top with onion rings during last 5 minutes.

Bunch O' Brunch

*"The LORD your God is with you.
. . . He will quiet you with his love."
(Zephaniah 3:17)*

Bunch 'o Brunch

Bunch 'o Brunch

There is something about brunch that triggers relaxation in our home. It may be because brunch is a variation from our regular schedule—not breakfast or lunch—but in between. Who knows? What I do know, however, is that we enjoy the following egg stratas at any time of day. And they're as easy as one, two, three!

• Basic Egg Strata •

8 slices firm bread, crusts removed, cubed
1/2 cup chopped onion
2 cups shredded cheddar cheese
10 large eggs
2 cups milk

Step One: Mix bread cubes, onion and cheese. Add salt and pepper according to taste. Put mixture in 13 x 9 x 2-inch baking dish that has been sprayed with cooking oil.

Step Two: Add meat, vegetables, etc., if desired, as indicated in the following recipes.

Step Three: Whisk together eggs and milk. Pour evenly over bread mixture.

Country Breakfast Strata

1 Basic Egg Strata
1/2 lb. cubed ham, cooked sausage or cooked,
    crumbled bacon

Assembly: Mix Basic Egg Strata to Step One. Add meat to bread mixture. Continue with Step Three by whisking together eggs and milk and pouring evenly over bread and meat mixture. Cover tightly with foil. Label. Freeze.

Preparation: Thaw. Bake uncovered at 350°F 45-50 minutes until set.

Easy Eggs Benedict

1 Basic Egg Strata (substitute 8 English muffin
    halves, torn, for bread)
1/2 lb. Canadian bacon or ham slices, cut in strips
1 package hollandaise sauce mix

Assembly: Mix Basic Egg Strata to Step One. Add meat to bread mixture. Continue with Step Three by whisking together eggs and milk and pouring evenly over bread and meat mixture. Cover tightly with foil. Attach sauce mix. Label. Freeze.

Preparation: Thaw. Bake uncovered at 350°F 45-50 minutes until set. While strata is baking, prepare hollandaise sauce mix according to package directions. Pour warm sauce over strata before serving.

Mexican Breakfast Strata

1 Basic Egg Strata
1/2 lb. cooked chorizo sausage
1/4 cup chopped green chilies (optional)

Assembly: Mix Basic Egg Strata to Step One. Add cooked meat and chilies (optional) to bread mixture. Continue with Step Three by whisking together eggs and milk and pouring evenly over bread and meat mixture. Cover tightly with foil. Label. Freeze.

Preparation: Thaw. Bake uncovered at 350°F 45-50 minutes until set. Serve with salsa, if desired.

Potato Strata

1 Basic Egg Strata (substitute 1 16-ounce package
   of frozen hash brown potatoes for bread cubes)
1/2 lb. cubed ham, cooked sausage or cooked,
   crumbled bacon

Assembly: Mix Basic Egg Strata to Step One. Add meat to frozen hash brown mixture. Continue with Step Three by whisking together eggs and milk and pouring evenly over potato/meat mixture. Cover tightly with foil. Label. Freeze.

Preparation: Thaw. Bake uncovered at 350°F 40-45 minutes.

Stuffed French Toast

1 Basic Egg Strata (omit cheddar cheese and onion
   and substitute cinnamon swirl bread for plain bread)
8 ounces cream cheese, cubed
1 large apple, peeled and chopped

Assembly: Mix Basic Egg Strata to Step One (omitting cheddar cheese and onion and substituting cinnamon swirl bread for plain bread). Add cheese and apple. Continue with Step Three by whisking together eggs and milk and pouring evenly over bread mixture. Cover tightly with foil. Label. Freeze.

Preparation: Thaw. Bake uncovered at 350°F 45-50 minutes until set. Sprinkle with powdered sugar and serve with maple or fruit syrup.

Perfect Poultry

"Then all the people went away to eat and drink . . . and to celebrate with great joy." (Nehemiah 8:12)

Perfect Poultry

Perfect Poultry

I remember the first time I roasted a turkey on a non-holiday. I was sliding the big bird into the oven on a Saturday morning in April as my children peered at me with that "Uh-oh, what's she up to now?" look. My youngest daughter, Anna, finally piped up, "I love Thanksgiving! How many days 'til Christmas, Mommy?"

These days, my family is accustomed to finding a frozen turkey or two among my groceries, especially right after Christmas when stores, trying to clear their shelves of leftover holiday birds, drastically reduce the prices. Not only is turkey a good buy, but it's also simple to roast, and the cooked meat is a perfect substitute in numerous dishes calling for cooked chicken. As an added bonus, the turkey frame makes a simply wonderful soup stock.

Whether you roast, boil, braise or grill, poultry (especially the white meat) is a healthy choice for your table.

• Basic Roast Chicken or Turkey •

3 whole chickens (2-3 lbs. each) or 1 turkey (9-10 lbs.)
1 large onion, cut into chunks
2 stalks celery, cleaned and cut into 2-3 inch chunks
cooking oil
poultry seasoning

Thoroughly rinse bird(s) with water inside and out. Rub with cooking oil and sprinkle with poultry seasoning. Stuff cavities loosely with onion and celery. Place bird(s) in oiled roasting pan. Tent pan with foil. Roast at 325°F until juices run clear and meat thermometer registers 165°. (Time will depend on size of the bird(s), but is generally 20 minutes per pound.) Remove bird(s) from pan. Allow to cool. Slice, cube or shred meat according to recipe needs. **Yield**: approximately 10 cups.

• Basic Stewed Chicken or Turkey •

3 whole chickens (3 lbs. each) or 1 turkey (9-10 lbs.)
1 large onion, cut into chunks
2 stalks celery, cleaned and cut into 2-3 inch chunks
1/2 t. poultry seasoning

Thoroughly rinse bird(s) with water inside and out. Cut into pieces and place bird(s) in large stock pot(s) with onion and celery. Cover with water. Add poultry seasoning. Simmer gently until meat is cooked but still juicy. Drain, reserving broth for soup stock, if desired. Allow meat to cool. Slice, cube or shred meat according to recipe needs. **Yield:** approximately 10 cups.

Easy Chicken Divan

3 cups sliced, cooked chicken or turkey
1 16-ounce package frozen broccoli
1 can cream of chicken soup
2/3 cup mayonnaise
1 t. lemon juice
1/2 cup shredded cheddar cheese
1 T. butter or margarine, melted
1/2 cup bread crumbs

Assembly: Spray 13 x 9 x 2-inch baking dish with cooking oil. Sprinkle frozen broccoli in bottom of pan. Top with chicken. Combine soup, mayonnaise and lemon juice. Spread over chicken. Top with cheese. Mix bread crumbs and melted butter. Sprinkle over casserole. Cover tightly with foil. Label. Freeze.

Preparation: Thaw. Bake uncovered at 350°F 25-30 minutes.

White Chili

1 T. minced garlic
1 1/2 cups chopped onions
1 T. oil
3 16-ounce cans Great Northern beans, drained
10 cups chicken broth
1 4-ounce can chopped green chilies, drained
2 16-ounce cans diced tomatoes
2 t. cumin
1 1/2 t. oregano
1/4 t. ground cloves
1/4 t. red pepper (or to taste)
4 cups cooked, shredded chicken or turkey
1 cup shredded jack cheese

Assembly: Sauté onions and garlic in oil. Cool. Place with remaining ingredients, except cheese, in 1-gallon freezer bag. Place cheese in a small self-sealing bag. Place both bags in 2-gallon self-sealing bag. Label. Freeze.

Preparation: Thaw. Simmer soup gently for at least 30-40 minutes. Serve garnished with cheese.

Chicken Pot Pie

3 cups cooked, cubed chicken or turkey

1 16-ounce package frozen mixed vegetables (corn, green
   beans, carrots)

2 10 1/2-ounce cans chicken gravy or 2 1/2 cups
   homemade gravy

Pantry:
1 tube large refrigerated biscuits

Assembly: Mix chicken, gravy and vegetables. Place in 1-gallon freezer bag. Label. Freeze.

Preparation: Thaw. Place in 2-quart casserole dish. Bake uncovered at 400°F 20 minutes.
Top with refrigerated biscuits. Bake 10-15 minutes longer.

Jambalaya

2 T. butter or margarine
2 cups chopped onions
1 cup chopped green pepper
2 t. minced garlic
3/4 lb. smoked sausage, sliced
2 16-ounce cans diced tomatoes
1/2 t. thyme
1/2 t. pepper
1/2 t. hot sauce (or to taste)
1 T. dried parsley flakes
1 cup chicken broth
1 cup tomato or vegetable juice
4 cups cooked and shredded chicken or turkey
3/4 cup rice, uncooked (regular, not parboiled)
1 lb. shelled, deveined shrimp, uncooked

Assembly: Sauté onions, green pepper and garlic in butter. Cool. Place in 1-gallon freezer bag with remaining ingredients, except rice and shrimp. Place rice and shrimp in separate 1-quart freezer bags. Place all bags in 2-gallon self-sealing bag. Label. Freeze.

Preparation: Thaw. Simmer soup gently for 20-30 minutes. Add rice and continue simmering another 15 minutes. Add shrimp, and cook for an additional 5 minutes, just until shrimp begin to turn pink and curl.

Chicken and Dumplings

3 cups cubed, cooked chicken or turkey
1 16-ounce package frozen mixed vegetables (corn,
    green beans, carrots)
6-7 cups chicken broth
1/2 t. poultry seasoning
1/2 t. onion powder
2 cups buttermilk baking mix
2/3 cup milk

Assembly: Place all ingredients except baking mix in 1-gallon freezer bag. Place bag in another 1-gallon bag to prevent leakage. Place baking mix in a smaller self-sealing bag. Place both bags in 2-gallon self-sealing bag. Label. Freeze.

Preparation: Thaw. Place soup mixture in a dutch-oven-sized pot. Bring to boil. Meanwhile, mix baking mix with 2/3 cup milk. Drop by spoonfuls into bubbling mixture and push down in broth. Cook uncovered 10 minutes and covered another 10 minutes.

Karen's Tortilla Soup

4 cups cooked, shredded chicken or turkey
2 16-ounce cans stewed tomatoes
2 16-ounce cans ranch-style beans
2 cups chicken broth
1 cup water
1 10-ounce can tomatoes with green chilies
1 cup chopped onions
1 package taco seasoning mix
1 package ranch dressing mix
1 16-ounce can hominy
1 cup shredded cheddar cheese
3 cups tortilla chips

Assembly: Place all ingredients except cheese and tortilla chips in 1-gallon freezer bag. Place in another 1-gallon bag to prevent leakage. Place cheese and chips in separate 1-quart freezer bags. Place all bags in 2-gallon self-sealing bag. Label. Freeze.

Preparation: Thaw. Simmer soup gently for at least 30-40 minutes. Serve garnished with cheese, chips and, if desired, sour cream and sliced green onions.

Swiss Casserole

3 cups cubed, cooked chicken or turkey
2 cups sliced celery
2 cups croutons
1 cup mayonnaise (may use light, if desired)
1 cup swiss cheese
1/2 t. salt
1/4 t. pepper
1/3 cup chopped walnuts

Assembly: Mix all ingredients except walnuts. Place in 1-gallon freezer bag. Place walnuts in a small self-sealing bag. Place both bags in 2-gallon self-sealing bag. Label. Freeze.

Preparation: Thaw. Place in 2-quart casserole dish. Sprinkle with walnuts. Bake uncovered at 350°F 30-35 minutes or until thoroughly heated.

Cheesy Chicken Broccoli

3 cups cubed, cooked chicken or turkey
2 cups chicken broth
2 cups frozen broccoli cuts
8 ounces processed cheese spread, cubed
1 cup parboiled white rice, uncooked

Assembly: Mix all ingredients except rice. Place in 1-gallon freezer bag. Place rice in separate small self-sealing bag. Place both bags in 2-gallon self-sealing bag. Label. Freeze.

Preparation: Thaw. Place chicken mixture in skillet. Bring to boil. Stir in rice. Cover. Remove from heat and let stand 5-7 minutes.

Three-Bean Turkey Soup

3 cups cooked, shredded chicken or turkey
1 16-ounce can red kidney beans, drained
1 16-ounce can black beans, drained
1 16-ounce can Great Northern beans, drained
1 T. oil
1/2 cup chopped onion
1/2 cup chopped green pepper
3/4 cup thinly sliced carrots
2 t. minced garlic
2 14-ounce cans stewed tomatoes with roasted garlic
    (plain stewed tomatoes will do, but the roasted garlic
    variety is wonderful!)
2 cups chicken broth
1 t. dried oregano leaves
1/2 t. dried thyme leaves
1 t. sugar
salt and pepper to taste

Assembly: Sauté onions, green pepper, carrots and garlic in oil. Cool. Place in 1-gallon freezer bag with remaining ingredients. Place bag in another 1-gallon bag to prevent leakage. Label. Freeze.

Preparation: Thaw. Simmer soup gently for at least 30-40 minutes before serving.

Chicken Tetrazzini

1 8-ounce package spaghetti, cooked *al dente*
3 cups cooked, cubed chicken or turkey
1 can cream of chicken soup
1/2 cup evaporated milk
1/2 cup grated Parmesan cheese

Assembly: Mix all ingredients. Place in 1-gallon freezer bag. Label. Freeze.

Preparation: Thaw. Place mixture in 11 x 7-inch casserole dish. Bake uncovered at 350°F 20-25 minutes or until thoroughly heated.

Hot Chicken Salad

3 cups cooked, cubed chicken or turkey
2 cups sliced celery
2 ounces sliced almonds
1/4 cup chopped onion
1/2 t. salt
3/4 cup mayonnaise (may use light, if desired)
1/2 cup shredded cheddar cheese
1/2 cup cornflakes

Assembly: Mix all ingredients except cheese and cornflakes. Place in 1-gallon freezer bag. Place cheese and cornflakes together in a small self-sealing bag. Crush bag to coarsely crush cornflakes. Place both bags in 2-gallon self-sealing bag. Label. Freeze.

Preparation: Thaw. Place chicken mixture in 11 x 7-inch casserole dish. Sprinkle with cornflake/cheese mixture. Bake uncovered at 350°F 25-30 minutes or until thoroughly heated.

Chicken Lasagna

8 ounces lasagna noodles, cooked *al dente*
1/2 cup chopped onion
1/2 cup chopped green pepper
1 cup sliced fresh mushrooms
2 T. butter or margarine
1 can cream of chicken soup
1/2 cup milk
1/2 t. dried basil
3 cups cooked, diced chicken or turkey
12 ounces ricotta cheese
1 egg or 1/4 cup egg substitute
1 1/2 cups shredded mozzarella cheese
1 1/2 cups shredded cheddar cheese

Assembly: Sauté onions, green pepper and mushrooms in butter or margarine. Add soup, milk, basil and chicken or turkey to vegetables. In separate bowl, mix ricotta, 1 cup mozzarella cheese and cheddar cheese. In a 13 x 9 x 2-inch baking dish that has been sprayed with cooking oil, spread 1 cup of sauce. Place three strips of pasta lengthwise over the sauce. Spread half of the ricotta mixture over the pasta. Cover with 1 1/2 cups sauce. Repeat layers of pasta, ricotta mixture and sauce. Top with remaining pasta, sauce and 1/2 cup mozzarella cheese. Cover tightly with foil. Label. Freeze.

Preparation: Thaw casserole. Bake covered at 350°F for 30 minutes. Remove foil and bake an additional 15 minutes until hot and bubbly. Let stand 10 minutes before serving.

Chicken Enchiladas

3 cups cooked, shredded chicken or turkey
1 31-ounce can refried beans
1 19-ounce can enchilada sauce
3 cups shredded cheddar or jack cheese
4 large flour tortillas cut or torn into strips

Assembly: Spray a 9 x 5-inch baking pan with cooking oil. Coat bottom of pan with thin layer of enchilada sauce. Layer 1/2 tortillas, chicken, beans and 1/3 cheese. Cover with 1/2 remaining enchilada sauce. Repeat layers with remaining tortillas, chicken, beans and sauce. Finish with remaining cheese. Cover tightly. Label. Freeze.

Preparation: Thaw. Bake at 350°, loosely covered until heated through. Serve with sour cream, salsa, sliced olives, chopped tomatoes and shredded lettuce, if desired.

Recipes to Be Made
with Uncooked Chicken

Orchard Chicken

4-6 boneless, skinless chicken breasts (uncooked)
1 package dry onion soup mix
1 16-ounce can apricots, drained (reserve juice)
1 16-ounce can peaches, drained (reserve juice)
1/2 cup reserved fruit juice
3 T. butter or margarine, cut into pieces
2 T. soy sauce

Assembly: Package chicken breasts in 1-gallon freezer bag. Process fruit, juice, butter (or margarine) and soy sauce in food processor or blender until smooth. Pour into a 1-quart freezer bag. Seal both bags, removing as much air as possible. Place both bags and onion soup mix in 2-gallon self-sealing bag. Label. Freeze.

Preparation: Thaw. Place chicken breasts in 13 x 9 x 2-inch baking dish which has been sprayed with cooking oil. Pour fruit sauce over chicken. Sprinkle soup mix on top of sauce. Bake covered at 350°F for 20 minutes. Remove, cover and bake another 15 minutes or until chicken is cooked through.

Mother's Wonderful Chicken

6 boneless, skinless chicken breast halves
2 cups herb-seasoned stuffing mix
6 slices Swiss cheese
1 10 1/2-ounce can cream of chicken soup
1 soup can water

Assembly: Put chicken breasts in bottom of casserole dish that has been sprayed with cooking oil. Place a slice of cheese over each breast. Sprinkle with stuffing mix. Whisk together soup and water. Pour over chicken. Cover tightly with foil. Freeze.

Preparation: Thaw. Bake uncovered at 350°F about 45-50 minutes.

Chicken Roll-Ups

6 boneless, skinless chicken breast halves,
    pounded to 1/2 inch thickness
salt and pepper
1 8-ounce tub whipped cream cheese with chives
6 slices bacon

Assembly: Season each chicken breast with salt and pepper and spread with 2-3 tablespoons of cream cheese. Roll up jellyroll style. Wrap one slice of bacon around each breast and tie with string. Place roll-ups on cookie sheet and quick-freeze for one hour (see Tip below). Place partially frozen breasts in 1-gallon freezer bag, removing as much air as possible. Label. Freeze.

Preparation: Place chicken breasts seam side down in shallow baking pan. Bake uncovered at 400°F about 40 minutes until chicken is tender and juices run clear. Broil just until bacon is crisp and golden.

Tip: Quick-freeze keeps items from sticking together when frozen. Just spread food on a baking sheet and place in the freezer. When frozen, package the items in a large freezer bag. The items will remain loose, allowing you to remove the exact number needed.

Chicken Cordon Bleu

6 boneless, skinless chicken breast halves,
    pounded to 1/2 inch thickness
6 slices Swiss cheese
6 slices ham (thin)
3 T. butter or margarine, melted
1/2 cup seasoned bread crumbs

Assembly: Place one slice of cheese and one slice of ham on each chicken breast. Roll up jellyroll style. Tie with string. Dip each breast in butter and then coat with crumbs. Place roll-ups on cookie sheet and quick freeze for one hour. Place partially frozen breasts in 1-gallon freezer bag, removing as much air as possible. Label. Freeze.

Preparation: Place chicken breasts seam side down in shallow baking pan. Bake uncovered at 400° about 40 minutes until chicken is tender and golden brown.

Sunday Chicken

Cooks while you are at church!

10 chicken thighs
1 box seasoned wild rice mix
1 10 1/2-ounce can cream of chicken soup
1 10 1/2-ounce can cream of mushroom soup
1 soup can water

Assembly: Remove skin from chicken. Put chicken pieces in bottom of casserole dish that has been sprayed with cooking oil. Whisk together soup, water and rice mix. Pour over chicken. Cover tightly with foil. Freeze.

Preparation: Thaw. Bake, tightly covered, at 350°F two hours; do not preheat oven.

Oven BBQ Chicken Dinner

6-8 chicken pieces, uncooked
1 1/2 cups barbeque sauce
4 ears corn (fresh or frozen)

Assembly: Package chicken pieces and corn in separate 1-gallon freezer bags. Place barbeque sauce in small self-sealing bag. Seal all bags, removing as much air as possible. Place bags in 2-gallon self-sealing bag. Label. Freeze.

Preparation: Thaw. Place chicken pieces in a 13 x 9 x 2-inch baking dish which has been sprayed with cooking oil. Spread barbeque sauce over chicken. Bake covered at 350°F for 20 minutes. Push chicken to one side of baking dish and arrange corn on opposite side. Bake uncovered another 20 minutes or until chicken is cooked through.

Skinny Fried Chicken

6 boneless, skinless chicken breast halves
1 1/2 cups cornflakes, crushed
1 t. cajun seasoning
2 egg whites
cooking spray

Assembly: Mix cornflakes and cajun seasoning. Dip each breast in egg white and then coat with crumb mixture. Place breasts on cookie sheet covered with wax paper and quick-freeze for one hour. Place partially frozen breasts in 1-gallon freezer bag, removing as much air as possible. Label. Freeze.

Preparation: Place frozen chicken in shallow baking pan coated with cooking spray. Spray chicken 2-3 times with cooking spray. Bake uncovered at 400°F about 10 minutes. Turn chicken over and spray each breast once again with cooking spray. Bake an additional 10 minutes or until done.

Bonus Roast

"She is clothed with strength and dignity; she can laugh at the days to come." (Proverbs 31:25)

Bonus Roast

Bonus Roast

In our family, a juicy pot roast is the ultimate in comfort food. Through the years, I've discovered that our Sunday roast is only the beginning for this versatile piece of meat. The basic recipe for Bonus Roast will give you a pot roast for your Sunday dinner as well as your choice of a number of dishes for a completely diffcrent taste.

• Bonus Roast •

4 lb. beef roast
1 package dry onion soup mix

Place roast in your Crock-Pot. Sprinkle with onion soup mix. Cover and cook on high 5 hours or low 8-10 hours. Chill, skim any fat from juices and slice meat. Use in recipes below.

Tip: Slicing meat is easier if you partially freeze it first.

Pot Roast with Carrots and Gravy

1/2 sliced Bonus Roast (with juices)
1 16-ounce package frozen baby carrots
beef broth (added to juices to make 1 1/2 cups)

Assembly: Place roast, carrots and broth in 1-gallon freezer bag. Seal bag, removing as much air as possible. Label. Freeze.

Preparation: Heat roast and carrots in broth until carrots reach desired degree of doneness. Remove to serving platter and keep warm. Whisk 2 T. flour into broth. Bring to boil, and cook until thickened. Pour gravy over roast or serve on the side.

Tip: Freezing cooked meat in a liquid, such as a sauce or broth, helps to keep meat from drying out.

Easy Sauerbraten

1/2 sliced Bonus Roast (with juices)
1 16-ounce package frozen baby carrots
beef broth (added to juices to make 1-1/2 cups)
1/4 cup red wine vinegar
1/4 t. cloves
1/3 cup gingersnap cookies, finely crushed

Pantry:
1/2 cup sour cream

Assembly: Place roast, carrots, broth, vinegar and cloves in 1-gallon freezer bag. Place crushed gingersnaps in a smaller self-sealing bag. Seal both bags, removing as much air as possible. Place both bags in 2-gallon self-sealing bag. Label. Freeze.

Preparation: Heat roast and carrots in broth until carrots reach desired degree of doneness. Remove to serving platter and keep warm. Whisk gingersnaps into broth. Bring to boil and cook until thickened. Stir in sour cream. Pour gravy over roast and vegetables.

BBQ Beef Sandwiches

1/2 sliced and chopped Bonus Roast (with juices)
3/4 cup favorite barbeque sauce
6 hamburger buns

Assembly: Place roast and barbeque sauce in 1-gallon freezer bag. Place buns in separate 1-gallon freezer bag. Seal both bags, removing as much air as possible. Place both bags in 2-gallon self-sealing bag. Label. Freeze.

Preparation: Heat roast in sauce until heated through. Serve on warm buns.

Philly Beef Sandwiches

1/2 sliced and chopped Bonus Roast (with juices)
1 medium onion, sliced
1 T. butter or margarine
1 T. Worcestershire sauce
1 cup shredded mozzarella cheese
6 hard rolls

Assembly: Sauté onions in butter until translucent. Add Worcestershire sauce. Place roast, onions and juices in 1-gallon freezer bag. Place buns in separate 1-gallon freezer bag. Put cheese in smaller self-sealing bag. Seal all bags, removing as much air as possible. Place all bags in 2-gallon self-sealing bag. Label. Freeze.

Preparation: Heat roast and onions in juices until heated through. Meanwhile, heat rolls in oven until slightly crispy. Split rolls, top with hot meat mixture and cheese.

Beefy Enchiladas

1/2 sliced, chopped Bonus Roast
1 31-ounce can refried beans
1 19-ounce can enchilada sauce
3 cups shredded cheddar or jack cheese
6-8 large flour tortillas cut or torn into strips

Assembly: Spray a 9 x 5-inch baking pan with cooking oil. Coat bottom of pan with enchilada sauce. Dip tortilla in enchilada sauce to soften. Spread 1/4 cup of beans on tortilla. Sprinkle meat and cheese on 1/2 of tortilla. Roll up. Place in baking dish, seam side down. Repeat with remaining tortillas, beans, meat and cheese (reserving 1 cup). Pour remaining enchilada sauce over all. Top with reserved cheese. Cover tightly with heavy-duty foil. Label. Freeze.

Preparation: Thaw. Bake loosely covered at 350°F until heated through. Serve with sour cream, salsa, sliced olives, chopped tomatoes and shredded lettuce, if desired.

Packets

"Her children arise and call her blessed; her husband also, and he praises her." (Proverbs 31:28)

Packets

Packets

Our family loves packet dinners! Not only are they delicious, but these little gems also can be slipped into the oven or onto the grill directly from the freezer. Since the food cooks inside the packet, there is no clean-up. Just crumble the foil and toss it in the trash. What more can you ask for?

Basic Instruction for Packets

1. Center ingredients on a sheet of heavy-duty aluminum foil. (For a main dish use a sheet 18 x 24 inches; for individual servings use a sheet 12 x 18 inches.)
2. Bring up the sides of the foil and make a double fold.
3. Double-fold both ends to form a packet. Be sure to leave room for heat to circulate inside. I generally place packets in a 2-gallon freezer bag to protect them from accidental puncture in the freezer. This also ensures that individual serving packets of the same kind are together.
4. Bake for indicated time on a cookie sheet or in a shallow roasting pan in 450°F oven; or cook on medium-high in a covered grill.
5. After cooking, carefully open the ends of the packet to allow steam to escape. Then open the top to remove food to serving dish.

Main Dish Packets

Sunday Roast

2 T. flour
3 lbs. boneless beef chuck roast
1 10 1/2-ounce can cream of mushroom soup
1 package dry onion soup mix
1 1/2 cups sliced mushrooms
2 cups frozen carrots

Assembly: Spray one side of 18 x 24-inch sheet of heavy-duty foil with cooking spray and coat with flour. Center roast and vegetables on foil. Mix soups and spread on top. Form packet. Place in 2-gallon freezer bag. Label. Freeze.

Preparation: Place in a roasting pan at least 2 inches deep. Bake at 400°F for 2-2 1/2 hours.

Backyard BBQ

2 T. flour
3 lbs. chicken pieces, skin removed
4 ears corn on the cob, halved (fresh or frozen)
1 medium onion, quartered
1 bag frozen baby carrots
2 t. garlic salt
1/2 t. lemon pepper (optional)
1/4 cup water

Assembly: Spray one side of 18 x 24-inch sheet of heavy-duty foil with cooking spray and coat with flour. Center chicken pieces in a single layer on foil. Mix spices and sprinkle on top of chicken. Place vegetables on top. Add 1/4 cup water. Form packet. Place in 2-gallon freezer bag. Label. Freeze.

Preparation: Place packet in a roasting pan at least 2 inches deep and bake at 450°F for 60-70 minutes, or place directly on covered grill, preheated to medium-high, for 40-45 minutes. Chicken is done when meat is no longer pink and juices run clear.

"Loosiana" Dinner

2 T. flour
1 lb. low-fat smoked sausage
    (turkey sausage or other)
1 lb. medium uncooked shrimp, peeled
4 ears corn on the cob, halved (fresh or frozen)
1 T. butter
2 t. cajun seasoning

Assembly: Spray one side of 18 x 24-inch sheet of heavy-duty foil with cooking spray and coat with flour. Center smoked sausage, shrimp and corn in center of foil. Sprinkle butter and spices on top. Form packet. Place in 2-gallon freezer bag. Label. Freeze.

Preparation: Place packet in a roasting pan at least 2 inches deep, and bake at 450°F for 20-25 minutes. Or place directly on covered grill, preheated to medium-high, for 15-20 minutes. Squeeze fresh lemon juice over all, if desired.

Individual Packets

Oriental Chicken

2 T. Flour
4 boneless, skinless chicken breasts
2 cups stir-fry frozen vegetables
1/2 cup stir-fry sauce

Assembly: For each packet, spray one side of 12 x 18-inch sheet of heavy-duty foil with cooking spray and coat with flour. Center one chicken breast and 1/2 cup vegetables on foil. Top with 2 T. stir-fry sauce. Form packet. Repeat to make a total of four packets. Place packets in 2-gallon freezer bag. Label. Freeze.

Preparation: Place packets on cookie sheet and bake at 450°F for 20-25 minutes. Or place directly on covered grill, preheated to medium-high, for 10-15 minutes. Be careful not to overcook. Chicken is done when meat is no longer pink.

Pesto Chicken

2 T. flour
4 boneless, skinless chicken breasts
2 cups Italian style frozen vegetables
4 T. pesto sauce

Assembly: For each packet, spray one side of 12 x 18-inch sheet of heavy-duty foil with cooking spray and coat with flour. Center one chicken breast on foil. Top chicken with 1 T. pesto sauce. Add 1/2 cup vegetables. Form packet. Repeat to make a total of four packets. Place packets in 2-gallon freezer bag. Label. Freeze.

Preparation: Place packets on cookie sheet and bake at 450° for 20-25 minutes. Or place directly on covered grill, preheated to medium high, for 10-15 minutes. Be careful not to overcook. Chicken is done when meat is no longer pink.

Salsa Chicken

2 T. flour
4 boneless, skinless chicken breasts
2 cups frozen corn
1 cup salsa

Assembly: For each packet, spray one side of 12 x 18-inch sheet of heavy-duty foil with cooking spray and coat with flour. Center one chicken breast and 1/2 cup vegetables on foil. Top with 1/4 cup salsa. Form packet. Repeat to make a total of four packets. Place packets in 2-gallon freezer bag. Label. Freeze.

Preparation: Place packets on cookie sheet and bake at 450° for 20-25 minutes. Or place directly on covered grill, preheated to medium high, for 10-15 minutes. Be careful not to overcook. Chicken is done when meat is no longer pink.

Italian Chicken

2 T. flour
4 boneless, skinless chicken breasts
1 cup marinara sauce (see page 87) or your favorite
  meatless spaghetti sauce
1 cup shredded mozzarella cheese

Assembly: For each packet, spray one side of 12 x 18-inch sheet of heavy-duty foil with cooking spray and coat with flour. Center one chicken breast and 1/4 cup sauce on foil. Top with 1/4 cup cheese. Form packet. Repeat to make a total of four packets. Place packets in 2-gallon freezer bag. Label. Freeze.

Preparation: Place packets on cookie sheet and bake at 450°F for 20-25 minutes. Or place directly on covered grill, preheated to medium-high, for 10-15 minutes. Be careful not to overcook. Chicken is done when meat is no longer pink.

Daily Bread

"Abigail lost no time. She took two hundred loaves of bread, two skins of wine, five dressed sheep, five seahs of roasted grain, a hundred cakes of raisins and two hundred cakes of pressed figs, and loaded them on donkeys." (1 Samuel 25:18)

Daily Bread

Daily Bread

It is verses in the Bible like the one you just read, describing the industrious Abigail, that once prompted me to avoid any recipe containing the word "knead." In fact, it wasn't until a realtor suggested that I slip a loaf of bread in the oven before a prospective buyer toured our home that I even attempted to bake frozen bread dough. "After all," the realtor chirped, "Nothing says 'Welcome home!' better than the smell of a loaf of fresh bread in the oven!"

Although I never would have admitted it at the time, I believe she was right. There are few things that can compare with the aroma and taste of fresh homemade bread. But between soccer games, swim lessons and committee meetings, who actually has time to make bread anymore? We all do! All it takes is a few minutes to do some advance planning and preparation—and perhaps investing in my favorite timesaving appliance, the bread machine!

I use my bread machine a lot! I bet you will too if you follow my lead and stockpile a variety of homemade bread mixes by measuring all the dry ingredients (except yeast) in plastic self-sealing bags. Next, label each bag with the name of the bread; then list the "wet" ingredients (water, butter, honey, etc.) and the amount of yeast needed for the recipe. (The bags can be reused next time you make up a batch of mixes.)

To use the mix, just measure the wet ingredients into your bread machine. Dump in your mix, add the yeast and turn it on! That's really all there is to it! In a few hours, you will be rewarded by the wonderful aroma of baking bread and a hot, flavorful loaf straight from the oven.

I have included a few of my favorite bread mixes on the following pages. I encourage you to use the system to make up mixes from your favorite recipes. It's also important to remember that bread machines may vary depending on the model and manufacturer. You may have better success, at least at first, with the recipes included in your instruction manual which were developed specifically for your machine. It's also important to add the ingredients in the order recommended by your machine.

When trying a new recipe, listen to your machine. If the machine sounds labored or the dough looks dry instead of a smooth satiny ball, add a little water a tablespoon at a time. If the dough is flat or appears wet, add some flour a tablespoon at a time. Remember, to get the best results from your bread machine, measure all ingredients accurately.

Honey White Bread

Assembly: For each mix, place the following ingredients in a 1-quart self-sealing bag:

3 cups bread flour
3/4 t. salt
2 T. dry milk

Preparation: Before starting your bread machine, add the following ingredients in the order given (or in the order suggested by the manufacturer):

1 1/4 cups warm water
3 T. honey
1-2 T. butter or margarine
bread mix
1 t. active dry yeast

Spicy Raisin Bread

Assembly: For each mix, place the following ingredients in a 1-quart self-sealing bag:

3 cups bread flour
2 T. dry milk
2 T. sugar
1 t. salt
1/4 t. each: cloves, allspice
1 t. cinnamon
1/2 cup raisins

Preparation: Before starting your bread machine, add the following ingredients in the order given (or in the order suggested by the manufacturer):

1 1/4 cups warm water
1-2 T. butter or margarine
bread mix
1 1/2 t. active dry yeast

NOTE: You can vary this recipe by eliminating the spices and raisins and adding dried fruit (apricots or cranberries) and nuts (walnuts, pecans, almonds).

Oatmeal Bread

Assembly: For each mix, place the following ingredients in a 1-quart self-sealing bag:

2 cups bread flour
1 cup oatmeal
2 T. dry milk
1 t. salt

Preparation: Before starting your bread machine, add the following ingredients in the order given (or in the order suggested by the manufacturer):

1 cup warm water
3 T. honey
1-2 T. butter or margarine
bread mix
2 t. active dry yeast

Honey Wheat Bread

Assembly: For each mix, place the following ingredients in a 1-quart self-sealing bag:

2 cups bread flour
1 cup whole wheat flour
2 T. dry milk
1 t. salt

Preparation: Before starting your bread machine, add the following ingredients in the order given (or in the order suggested by the manufacturer):

1 cup warm water
3 T. honey
1-2 T. butter or margarine
bread mix
2 t. active dry yeast

Italian Herb Bread

Assembly: For each mix, place the following ingredients in a 1-quart self-sealing bag:

3 cups bread flour
2 T. dry milk
1 1/2 t. salt
1 t. each: basil, oregano, parsley, garlic powder

Preparation: Before starting your bread machine, add the following ingredients in the order given (or in the order suggested by the manufacturer):

1 1/4 cups warm water
1-2 T. butter or margarine
bread mix
2 t. active dry yeast

Spicy Cornmeal Bread

Assembly: For each mix, place the following ingredients in 1-quart self-sealing bag:

2 cups bread flour
1 cup cornmeal
2 T. dry milk
1 1/2 t. salt
2 T. sugar

Preparation: Before starting your bread machine, add the following ingredients in the order given (or in the order suggested by the manufacturer):

3/4 cup warm water
1/2 cup salsa
1-2 T. butter or margarine
bread mix
2 t. active dry yeast

Mrs. Salzmann's Cinnamon Rolls

This recipe was always a big hit with my son's Sunday school class. It is amazing how the promise of a gooey roll at the end of class can calm even the most restless adolescent boy. The rolls are a bit fussy to make, but well worth the extra time.

Assembly: For each mix, place the following ingredients in a 1-quart self-sealing bag:

4 cups all-purpose flour
3 T. sugar
1 t. salt

Preparation: Before starting your bread machine, add the following ingredients in the order given (or in the order suggested by the manufacturer):

1 1/3 cups warm milk
2 T. butter or margarine
2 eggs
bread mix
2 t. active dry yeast

Run bread machine on dough cycle. When cycle is complete, remove dough from machine to a floured surface. Punch dough down and let rest about 10 minutes. While dough rests, cream together the following ingredients to make filling:

3/4 cup brown sugar
1/4 cup flour
1 T. cinnamon
1/2 cup butter (softened)

After dough has rested, roll it out to form a 9 x 12-inch rectangle. Spread dough with the filling mixture and roll up jellyroll style. Slice roll into 1-inch pieces, and place cut side up in a greased 9 x 13-inch pan. Let rolls rise in a warm place until double in size (or cover the pan and place in the refrigerator for 2-24 hours. Remove 30 minutes before baking to bring rolls to room temperature.)

Before baking, pour over top of rolls:

1 cup heavy cream (or half and half)

Bake rolls at 375°F for 25 minutes or until golden brown.
Frost with a butter or vanilla frosting (I use canned frosting). Rolls are best served warm and gooey but are delicious anytime, any way—and anywhere.

SECTION THREE

Boot Camp

Getting
Started

Getting Started
Menu Plans, Grocery Lists
and Game Plans

You've read the book, reviewed the recipes and are convinced that using *The Occasional Cook* system will save you time and money. Still . . . the thought of preparing meals for an entire month in one sitting is a bit intimidating. Don't worry—you are not alone. Many cooks, including myself, have felt the same way. For this reason, I have included several meal plans of varying complexity to help you "ease" into the system. Once you get the hang of cooking in bulk, you'll never be intimidated by a ten-pound package of hamburger again!

MENU PLANS

Seven Meals—Ground Beef

Next time ground beef is on sale at the market, set aside an afternoon to put together these family-pleasing meals! If the meals are a hit with your family, why not save even more time and money by doubling each recipe?

1. Nebraska Shepherd's Pie (p. 49)
2. Porcupines (p. 52)
3. Swedish Meatballs (over noodles) (p. 54)
4. Chuck Wagon Quesadillas (p. 59)
5. Taco Soup (p. 63)
6. Tastee Joes (p. 64)
7. BBQ Cups (p. 64)

GAME PLAN

Prep Work

1. Make fresh bread crumbs (see tip on page 22).
2. Chop onions.
3. Shred carrots.
4. Chop dill pickle.

Meal Assembly

1. Assemble Basic Ground Meat Mixture (uncooked) p. 45. (3x)
2. Mix, shape and bake meatballs for Porcupines and Swedish Meatballs.
3. While meatballs cook and cool, assemble and package Nebraska Shepherd's Pie.
4. Assemble sauces for Swedish Meatballs and Porcupines and package with cool meatballs. (NOTE: Since Swedish Meatballs will be served over noodles, place package of meatballs and sauce and unopened package of frozen noodles together in a 2-gallon self-sealing bag.)
5. Assemble and cook Basic Ground Meat Mixture (cooked). (4x) p. 56.
6. Assemble and package Chuck Wagon Quesadillas.
7. Assemble and package Taco Soup.
8. Assemble and package Tastee Joes.
9. Assemble and package BBQ Cups.
10. Prepare meal inventory (see page 23).

GROCERY LIST
(Seven Meals—Ground Beef)

Bread/Rolls

- 2 1/4 cups fresh bread crumbs (see tip on page 22)
- 1/4 cup white rice (not Minute Rice)
- 4 flour tortillas (12-inch)
- 6 hamburger buns
- 4 cups tortilla chips

Dairy

- 3 eggs
- 1 cup milk
- 4 1/2 cups shredded cheddar cheese
- 2 packages large (or giant-sized) refrigerated biscuits

Frozen

- 1/2 package frozen mashed potatoes (or 3 cups fresh)
- 12-ounce package frozen mixed country vegetables
- 3 cups frozen corn
- 10-ounce package frozen egg noodles

Meat

- 8 1/2 lbs. lean ground beef

Pantry

- 1 cup catsup
- 4 1/2 cups beef broth
- 1 6-ounce can tomato paste
- 1/2 cup dill pickles (2-3 spears)
- 1 10 1/2-ounce can cream of mushroom soup
- 1 9-ounce can baked beans
- 1 16-ounce can diced tomatoes

- 2 12-ounce cans diced tomatoes with chilies
- 2 16-ounce cans kidney beans
- 1 1/8 cups barbeque sauce
- 1 envelope taco seasoning mix

Fresh Produce

- 2 large onions
- 3 carrots
- 4 t. minced garlic
- 1 small head red cabbage (used on day meal is served)

Packaging

- 2-gallon self-sealing freezer bags (6)
- 1-gallon self-sealing freezer bags (11)
- 1-quart self-sealing freezer bags (5)

Staples

- sugar (1 T.)
- brown sugar (1/3 cup)
- white vinegar (1 T.)
- red wine vinegar (1/4 cup)
- mustard (1 t.)

Spices

- salt (1 t.)
- pepper (3/4 t.)
- ground nutmeg (1/4 t.)
- chili powder (1 t.)
- ground cumin (1 t.)
- sage leaves (1 t.)

Seven Meals—Chicken or Turkey

Remember that extra holiday turkey hiding in the back of your freezer? Or the good deal you found on chicken but have no idea what to do with it? Here's your opportunity to turn your quandary into some wonderful meals in just a few hours!

1. Easy Chicken Divan (p. 104)
2. Chicken and Dumplings (p. 108)
3. Karen's Tortilla Soup (p. 109)
4. Hot Chicken Salad (p. 112)
5. Chicken Enchiladas (p. 114)
6. Sunday Chicken (p. 116)
7. Chicken Breasts with Citrus Marinade (pp. 40-41)

GAME PLAN

Prep Work

1. Chop 1 1/2 onions.
2. Chunk 1 1/2 onion.
3. Cut 3 stalks celery into 2- to 3-inch chunks.
4. Slice remaining celery.
5. Prepare Basic Stewed Chicken, pg. 104 (1.5x). (NOTE: You can substitute a roasted turkey or chickens for the cooked poultry in these recipes.)
6. Remove meat from bones when birds are cool. Strain reserved broth. Skim fat after broth has chilled.

Meal Assembly

1. Assemble and package Easy Chicken Divan.
2. Assemble and package Chicken and Dumplings.
3. Assemble and package Karen's Tortilla Soup.
4. Assemble and package Hot Chicken Salad.
5. Assemble and package Chicken Enchiladas.
6. Assemble and package Sunday Chicken using raw chicken pieces. (NOTE: If chicken is frozen, do not thaw and refreeze.)
7. Assemble Citrus Marinade and package with frozen chicken breasts.
8. Prepare meal inventory (see page 23).

GROCERY LIST
(Seven Meals—Chicken or Turkey)

Bread/Rolls

- 1/2 cup fresh bread crumbs (see tip on page 22)
- 4 flour tortillas (12-inch)
- 3 cups tortilla chips

Dairy

- 5 cups shredded cheddar cheese
- 2/3 cup milk
- 1 T. butter or margarine

Frozen

- 12-ounce package frozen mixed country vegetables
- 12-ounce package frozen broccoli

Meat

- 5 whole chickens (2-3 lbs. each)
- 10 chicken thighs
- 4-6 boneless, skinless chicken breasts (frozen)

Pantry

- 9 cups chicken broth
- 1 package wild rice mix
- 1 10 1/2-ounce can cream of mushroom soup
- 2 10 1/2-ounce cans cream of chicken soup
- 2 16-ounce cans ranch-style beans
- 1 19-ounce can enchilada sauce
- 2 15 1/2-ounce cans refried beans
- 2 16-ounce cans stewed tomatoes
- 1 10-ounce can diced tomatoes with chilies
- 1 16-ounce can hominy
- 1 package ranch dressing mix
- 1 envelope taco seasoning mix
- 2 cups buttermilk baking mix

Fresh Produce

- 2 ounces sliced almonds

Fresh Produce

- 3 large onions
- 7 stalks celery

Packaging

- 2-gallon self-sealing freezer bags (3)
- 1-gallon self-sealing freezer bags (5)
- 1-quart self-sealing freezer bags (4)
- 13 x 9-inch baking dishes—glass or disposable (3)
- heavy duty foil

Staples

- sugar
- lemon juice (5 T.)
- lime juice (2 T.)
- orange juice (4 T.)
- vegetable oil (3 T.)
- mayonnaise (1/3 cup)
- salad dressing (1/2 cup)
- cornflakes (or other unsweetened cereal) (1/2 cup)
- cooking spray

Spices

- salt (1/2 t.)
- cilantro (fresh or dried) (1 T.)
- poultry seasoning (1 t.)
- onion powder (1/2 t.)

Fourteen Meals

You've earned your cooking stripes! At the end of the day you'll be able to make:

1. Italian Meat Loaf (p. 47)
2. BBQ Meatballs (p. 54)
3. Zesty Burgers (p. 55)
4. Easy Enchiladas (p. 60)
5. Captain's Stew (p. 62)
6. Italian Biscuit Cups (p. 65)
7. Spaghetti with Sugo Sauce (p. 88)
8. Old-Fashioned Lasagna (p. 92)
9. Potato Strata (p. 99)
10. Stuffed French Toast (p. 99)
11. White Chili (p. 105)
12. Cheesy Chicken Broccoli (p. 110)
13. Chicken Tetrazzini (p. 112)
14. Chicken Breasts with Honey Mustard Marinade (pp. 40-41)

GAME PLAN

Prep Work

1. Make fresh bread crumbs (see tip on page 22).
2. Chunk 1 onion and chop remaining onions.
3. Cut 2 stalks celery into 2- to 3-inch chunks.
4. Shred carrots.
5. Assemble, simmer and cool Basic Marinara Sauce (1x). p. 87.
6. Prepare Basic Stewed Chicken (1x) p. 104. (NOTE: You can substitute a roasted turkey or chickens for the cooked poultry in these recipes.)

7. Remove meat from bones when birds are cool. Strain reserved broth. Skim fat after broth has chilled.

Meal Assembly

1. Assemble Basic Ground Meat Mixture (uncooked) (3x) p. 45.
2. Mix, shape and bake meatballs for BBQ Meatballs.
3. While meatballs cook and cool, assemble and package Italian Meat Loaf.
4. Assemble and package Zesty Burgers.
5. Assemble and cook Basic Ground Meat Mixture (cooked) (4x). p. 56.
6. While ground beef cools, assemble and package Captain's Stew.
7. Assemble and package BBQ Meatballs with cool meatballs.
8. Assemble and package Easy Enchiladas.
9. Assemble and package Italian Biscuit Cups.
10. Boil noodles for Old-Fashioned Lasagna. (NOTE: Cook pasta only to al dente. Do not overcook.)
11. Meanwhile, brown Italian sausage, drain and cool.
12. While Italian sausage cools, assemble and package Old Fashioned Lasagna.
13. Assemble and package Spaghetti with Sugo Sauce with cool Italian sausage.
14. Assemble and package Potato Strata.
15. Assemble and package Stuffed French Toast.
16. Boil spaghetti for Chicken Tetrazzini. (NOTE: Cook pasta only to al dente. Do not overcook.)
17. Meanwhile, assemble and package White Chili.

18. Assemble and package Cheesy Chicken Broccoli.
19. Assemble and package Chicken Tetrazzini.
20. Assemble Honey Mustard Marinade and package with frozen chicken breasts.
21. Prepare meal inventory (see p. 23).

GROCERY LIST
Fourteen Meals

Bread/Rolls

- 2 1/4 cups fresh bread crumbs (see tip on page 22)
- 4 flour tortillas (12-inch)
- 4 hamburger buns
- 8 slices cinnamon swirl bread

Dairy

- 5 cups shredded cheddar cheese
- 1 cup shredded jack cheese
- 3 1/2 cups shredded mozzarella cheese
- 12 ounces ricotta cheese
- 3/4 cup Parmesan cheese
- 2 packages large (or giant-sized) refrigerated biscuits
- 2 dozen eggs
- 8-ounce package cream cheese
- 8 ounces processed cheese
- 5 1/4 cups milk

Frozen

- 12-ounce package frozen mixed country vegetables
- 12-ounce package frozen broccoli
- 16-ounce package frozen hash browns

Meat

- 8 1/2 lbs. lean ground beef
- 3 whole chickens (3 lbs. each)
- 6 boneless, skinless chicken breasts (frozen)

- 1 lb. Italian sausage
- 1/2 lb. ham steak, cubed

Pantry

- 12 cups chicken broth
- 4 cups beef broth
- 1 10-ounce can cream of chicken soup
- 1 cup barbeque sauce
- 1 19-ounce can enchilada sauce
- 2 15 1/2-ounce cans refried beans
- 3 16-ounce cans diced tomatoes
- 1 6-lb. 4-ounce can crushed tomatoes
- 1 6-lb. 4-ounce can diced tomatoes
- 1 14-ounce can tomato paste
- 1 16-ounce can kidney beans
- 3 16-ounce cans Great Northern beans
- 1 4-ounce can diced green chilies
- 8 ounces vegetable juice (V-8, etc.)
- 2 8-ounce packages spaghetti
- 1 8-ounce package lasagna noodles
- 4 ounces evaporated milk
- 1 cup parboiled rice

Fresh Produce

- 6 large onions
- 2 stalks celery
- 2 carrots
- 6-7 tablespoons minced garlic
- 1 large apple
- 9 cloves garlic, crushed

GROCERY LIST (continued)
Fourteen Meals

Packaging

- 2-gallon self-sealing freezer bags (6)
- 1-gallon self-sealing freezer bags (13)
- 1-quart self-sealing freezer bags (6)
- 13 x 9-inch baking dishes—glass or disposable (4)
- heavy duty foil

Staples

- olive oil (3 T.)
- sugar (2 1/2 t.)
- Dijon mustard (1/3 cup)
- honey (1/2 cup)
- soy sauce (1/4 cup)
- lemon juice (4 T.)
- vegetable oil (1 T.)
- cooking spray
- prepared horseradish (1 T.)

Spices

- salt (3-4 t.)
- pepper (3-4 t.)
- poultry seasoning (1/2 t.)
- cumin (2 t.)
- paprika (1/2 t.)
- marjoram (1 t.)
- oregano (4 T.)
- thyme (1 t.)
- fennel seed (2 t.)
- dried parsley (2 t.)
- basil (3 T.)
- ground cloves (1/4 t.)
- red pepper (1/4 t.)

Twenty-One Meals

You have come through boot camp with flying colors, earned your cooking stripes and are fully equipped to do battle in the kitchen. Don't let that mountain of hamburger intimidate you! Freedom waits!

1. Savory Meat Loaf (p. 46)
2. Italian Meatball Grinders (p. 51)
3. Cheeseburger Casserole (p. 56)
4. Popover Pizza (p. 57)
5. Mexi-Melt (p. 58)
6. Taco Soup (p. 63)
7. Tastee Joes (p. 64)
8. Spaghetti with Meatballs (p. 88)
9. Baked Pasta (p. 91)
10. Easy Chicken Divan (p. 104)
11. Chicken and Dumplings (p. 108)
12. Swiss Casserole (p. 110)
13. Three-Bean Turkey Soup (p. 111)
14. Chicken Enchiladas (p. 114)
15. Orchard Chicken (p. 114)
16. Sunday Chicken (p. 116)
17. Oven BBQ Chicken Dinner (p. 117)
18. Pot Roast with Carrots and Gravy (p. 121)
19. BBQ Beef Sandwiches (p. 122)
20. Salsa Chicken (p. 130)
21. Italian Chicken (p. 131)

GAME PLAN

Prep Work

1. Prepare Bonus Roast (p. 121) using Crock-Pot (1x). (NOTE: I often start the roast when I go to bed and let it cook overnight.)
2. Make fresh bread crumbs (see tip on page 22).
3. Chunk 1 1/2 onions and chop remaining onions.
4. Chop green pepper.
5. Cut 3 stalks celery into 2- to 3-inch chunks.
6. Shred carrots.
7. Assemble, simmer and cool Basic Marinara Sauce (1x). p. 87.
8. Prepare Basic Stewed Chicken (1 1/2x). p. 104. (NOTE: You can substitute roasted turkey or chickens for the cooked poultry in these recipes.)
9. Remove meat from bones when birds are cool. Strain reserved broth. Skim fat after broth has chilled.

Meal Assembly

1. Put cooked Bonus Roast in refrigerator to cool.
2. Assemble Basic Ground Meat Mixture (uncooked) (3x). p. 45.
3. Mix, shape and bake meatballs for Italian Meatball Grinders and Spaghetti and Meatballs. (NOTE: Meatball recipe is the same for both dishes.)
4. While meatballs cook and cool, assemble and package Savory Meat Loaf.
5. Assemble and cook Basic Ground Meat Mixture (cooked) (5x). p. 56.
6. Boil macaroni for Cheeseburger Casserole. (NOTE: Cook pasta only to *al dente*. Do not overcook.)
7. While ground beef cools, assemble Italian Meatball Grinders and Spaghetti and Meatballs using cool meatballs.

8. Assemble and package Cheeseburger Casserole.
9. Assemble and package Popover Pizza.
10. Assemble and package Mexi-Melt.
11. Assemble and package Taco Soup.
12. Assemble and package Tastee Joes.
13. Assemble and package Easy Chicken Divan.
14. Assemble and package Chicken and Dumplings.
15. Assemble and package Swiss Casserole.
16. Assemble and package Three-Bean Turkey Soup.
17. Assemble and package Chicken Enchiladas.
18. Boil noodles for Baked Pasta. (NOTE: Cook pasta only to *al dente*. Do not overcook.)
19. Assemble and package Orchard Chicken.
20. Assemble and package Sunday Chicken.
21. Assemble and package Oven BBQ Chicken Dinner.
22. Assemble and package Baked Pasta using cooled noodles.
23. Slice Bonus Roast and use meat and juices to assemble Pot Roast with Carrots and Gravy and BBQ Beef Sandwiches.
24. Assemble and package Salsa Chicken packets.
25. Assemble and package Italian Chicken packets.
26. Prepare meal inventory (see p. 23).

GROCERY LIST
(Twenty-One Meals)

Bread/Rolls
- 2 3/4 cups fresh bread crumbs (see tip on page 22)
- 4 flour tortillas (12-inch)
- 12 hamburger buns
- 4 hoagie rolls
- 8 cups tortilla chips
- 2 cups seasoned croutons

Dairy
- 5 1/2 cups shredded cheddar cheese
- 5 cups shredded mozzarella cheese
- 12 ounces ricotta cheese
- 3/4 cup Parmesan cheese
- 1 tube refrigerated crescent rolls
- 4 eggs
- 8 ounces processed cheese (Velveeta, etc.)
- 6 slices swiss cheese
- 1 1/2 cups milk
- 4 T. butter or margarine

Frozen
- 16-ounce package frozen mixed country vegetables
- 16-ounce package frozen broccoli
- 4 cups frozen corn
- 4 ears frozen corn on the cob
- 16-ounce package frozen baby carrots

Meat
- 9 1/2 lbs. lean ground beef
- 5 whole chickens (2-3 lbs. each)
- 14 boneless, skinless chicken breasts (frozen)

GROCERY LIST (continued)
Twenty-One Meals

- 18 chicken thighs or other meaty pieces
- 4-lb. beef roast (can use any cut, but rump or eye of round are lean choices)

Pantry

- 9 cups chicken broth
- 3 cups beef broth
- 1 package wild rice mix
- 1 envelope taco seasoning mix
- 2 cups buttermilk baking mix
- 2 envelopes dry onion soup mix
- 2 10-ounce cans cream of chicken soup
- 1 10-ounce can cream of mushroom soup
- 2-1/4 cups barbeque sauce
- 1 19-ounce can enchilada sauce
- 3 15 1/2-ounce cans refried beans
- 2 14-ounce cans diced tomatoes
- 2 16-ounce cans stewed tomatoes
- 1 6-lb. 4-ounce can crushed tomatoes
- 1 6-lb. 4-ounce can diced tomatoes
- 1 14-ounce can tomato paste
- 3 16-ounce cans kidney beans
- 1 16-ounce can black beans
- 1 16-ounce cans Great Northern beans
- 1 16-ounce can diced tomatoes with chilies
- 1 16-ounce can apricots
- 1 16-ounce can sliced peaches
- 1 8-ounce package spaghetti
- 1 8-ounce package penne pasta
- 1 8-ounce package elbow macaroni
- 1 cup chow mein noodles
- 1 1/2 cups salsa
- 1/3 cup chopped walnuts

Fresh Produce

- 7 large onions
- 1 small green pepper
- 5 stalks celery
- 4 carrots
- 8 T. minced garlic

Packaging

- 2-gallon self-sealing freezer bags (13)
- 1-gallon self-sealing freezer bags (22)
- 1-quart self-sealing freezer bags (9)
- 13 x 9-inch baking dishes—glass or disposable (4)
- heavy duty foil

Staples

- vegetable oil (1 T.)
- sugar (4 T.)
- brown sugar (1 T.)
- catsup (1 3/4 cups)
- mustard (2 T.)
- soy sauce (1/8 cup)
- lemon juice (1 T.)
- olive oil (3 T.)
- mayonnaise (2/3 cup)
- vinegar (1 T.)
- cooking spray

Spices

- salt (5 T.)
- pepper (4 1/2 t.)
- poultry seasoning (1 1/4 t.)
- oregano (4 T.)
- thyme (1/2 t.)
- fennel seed (4 t.)
- basil (3 T.)

You may request information regarding additional resources as well as Cyndy's workshops and seminars by writing to:

Cyndy Salzmann
c/o Family Haven Ministries
15905 Jones Circle
Omaha, Nebraska 68118
or call (402) 334-1565.

www.familyhavenministries.com

Notes

Notes

Notes

Notes

Notes

Notes

Notes

Notes

Notes

Notes